PRAISE FOR

The Power of Your Words

Robert Morris has beautifully wed the practical with the profound.
When we master our mouths, God blesses our lives. This book is in-depth
and scripturally sound. Yet even more, these pages hold the truest privilege
of a Spirit-led life—our ability to bless and release life.

LISA BEVERE
AUTHOR, *FIGHT LIKE A GIRL* AND *KISSED THE GIRLS AND MADE THEM CRY*

Robert Morris gives incredible insight on how your words can affect you
and the people around you, for better or for worse. Packed with powerful
principles, *The Power of Your Words* will help you understand the real meaning
of your words and give you practical suggestions on how to use them.

MIKE BRISKY
FORMER PGA TOUR PLAYER
ASSOCIATE PASTOR, GATEWAY CHURCH

Robert Morris once again hits the mark. In fact, he hits several in this book.
The Power of Your Words sheds light on how our words always have consequences.
Robert's encouraging style gives us hope that through the power of the
Holy Spirit any Christian can find victory over the powerful weapon that
is our tongue. He delivers spiritual truth in an entertaining, down-to-earth
manner that any reader, at any stage in his or her spiritual life—
unsaved to theologian—can appreciate.

CHAD HENNINGS
THREE-TIME SUPER BOWL CHAMPION, DALLAS COWBOYS
FORMER AIR FORCE FIGHTER PILOT

The Power of Your Words will take you beyond learning to living. I can attest
that if you embrace them as I did, your life will never be the same.
I believe that these life-changing principles taught by Robert Morris
will even break through denominational walls.

PETER HIRSCH
BEST-SELLING AUTHOR
MESSIANIC RABBI
EXECUTIVE PASTOR, GATEWAY CHURCH

Robert Morris has done the Body of Christ a great favor with this book. He skillfully manages to dig deeply into our attitudes and the words we use with one another in a kind and sensitive manner. Every Christian on the face of the earth needs to read this message. Thank you, Robert. *The Power of Your Words* is destined to be a classic.

CINDY JACOBS
FOUNDER, GENERALS INTERNATIONAL

It is with great excitement that I recommend Robert Morris's book, *The Power of Your Words*. Its message is a key to unlock our understanding about the significance of what we say. Our avowed enemy, Satan, doesn't want us to have a correct revelation about our words; he wants to keep us blinded so that he can use our words against us. But God wants us to know how to use words so that we can bless others and be blessed. Frankly, I have never read a book like this. As a result, it is my intention to buy copies of *The Power of Your Words* for each of my immediate family and for the hundreds of employees at Daystar. I strongly encourage you to get this book and then get copies of it for the people who are most important to you.

MARCUS D. LAMB
PRESIDENT AND CEO, DAYSTAR TELEVISION NETWORK

Pastor Robert Morris has written a book that will bring you closer to the heart of God and take you deeper into the Word of God. *The Power of Your Words* will make you aware of everything that you are saying and the lasting effect those words will have. The tongue is a powerful tool for Kingdom living.

TOMMY MADDOX
NFL QUARTERBACK, PITTSBURGH STEELERS
FOUNDER, TOMMY MADDOX FOUNDATION

We often take our speech for granted and fail to realize its value and effect. But the Bible has a lot to say about the power of the tongue. In *The Power of Your Words*, Robert Morris focuses our attention on the significance of each word we choose to express. It's time for us, the Church, to be accountable for the spiritual, mental and emotional events we set in motion with our words, both in our lives and in the lives of those around us. Robert effectively inspires and challenges us to exercise wisdom when speaking.

JAMES ROBISON
FOUNDER AND PRESIDENT, LIFE OUTREACH INTERNATIONAL

The Power of Your Words

Robert Morris

BETHANYHOUSE
a division of Baker Publishing Group
Minneapolis, Minnesota

Published by Bethany House Publishers
Minneapolis, Minnesota
www.bethanyhouse.com

Bethany House Publishers is a division of
Baker Publishing Group, Grand Rapids, Michigan

Bethany House edition published 2014
ISBN 978-0-7642-1712-8

Previously published by Regal Books

Printed in the United States of America

The Library of Congress has cataloged the original edition as follows:
    Morris, Robert (Robert Preston).
    The power of your words / Robert Morris.
        p. cm.
    ISBN 0-8307-3833-9 (trade paper) – ISBN 0-8307-3832-0 (international trade paper)
    1. Oral communication—Religious aspects—Christianity. 2. Communication—Religious aspects—Christianity.   I. Title.
    BV4597.53.C64M67 2006
    241'.672—dc22   2006002897

Baker Publishing Group publications use paper produced from sustainable forestry practices and post-consumer waste whenever possible.

23   24   25   26   27   28   29   15   14   13   12   11   10

Dedication

This book is dedicated to Jimmy Evans, my pastor, brother, mentor and friend, from whom I first learned these truths. Jimmy and his wonderful wife, Karen, host *Marriage Today*, one of the most effective marriage ministries I know. I encourage everyone who reads this book to watch and support *Marriage Today*.

Contents

Foreword

I was standing beside a swimming pool near the banks of the Mississippi River the day *"It"* happened to me.

I was 30 years old at the time. I had been raised in church, knew Christ and had a reasonably effective ministry; but *"It"* still hadn't happened to me.

I hope "It" doesn't sound casual or trivial, because I see *"It"* as one of the most essential foundational experiences a person can have. By "It," I'm referring to the God-graced gift of suddenly understanding the power of my spoken words—of how I use words, or fail to use them.

To this day, I'm grateful for the person God used to open that door of understanding. His name was Roy Hicks; and my "getting *It*" didn't take long—we only had a 30-minute conversation! But that half-hour placed in my hands one of the keys to living life on God's terms and, by His wisdom, acquiring a grasp of a pivotal life-transforming principle with life-giving power.

Has "It" happened to you? This book is your opportunity for such an encounter. It is a clearly communicated, wisely presented, pastorally written handbook that I believe could be to you what Roy was to me—an instrument relaying truth to heart and mind. Herein lies more than information: This book provides understanding so that a balanced and practical life application of a central Bible principle may become yours.

Robert Morris is a young leader I trust because of his pursuit to lead his flock with wise, biblical balance and to model a warm passion for godly, Spirit-filled living. As a pastor, he is a faithful shepherd—focused on serving his people, not on serving himself. His leadership reveals a passion to glorify Jesus Christ, a priority on worship, a life centered in God's Word and an even-handed, sensible openness to the full life-flow of the Holy Spirit in his own life and in the Church's.

So let me urge you to open God's Word as you take this book in hand. You'll find that what is said *here* is faithful to what is said *there*! As truth ignites faith, and wisdom is joined to understanding, you will be enriched. Here is teaching that will help you see the scope of Jesus' meaning when He said, "For by your words you will be justified, and by your words you will be condemned" (Matt. 12:37). Whatever *positive* comments you've ever heard about the principles and power of "faith's confession," this book is as good as it gets!

On the other hand, if you are aware—as I am—that some have distorted that wonderful truth, and that exaggerations and imbalance have caused others to be turned off if they even hear the expression, please hear me: *Whatever negative comments you've heard, this book corrects error, clarifies principles, focuses the truth, resolves questions and removes confusion.*

So, dear friend, step into these pages and you'll be escorted by a faithful teacher to find spiritual inspiration that can only flow from the anointing of the Holy Spirit at work—He who takes the things of Jesus, the Ultimate Teacher, and shows them unto us—doing what Jesus said He would do (see John 16:14).

Jack W. Hayford
Chancellor, The King's College and Seminary
Founding Pastor, The Church On The Way

February 2006
Los Angeles, California

Preface

For some, the assertions I am making about words having the ability to speak life or death will cause them to wonder if I'm espousing a doctrine that in the past has derisively been labeled "name it and claim it," "blab it and grab it," "confess it and possess it," or a multitude of other clever mockeries. The answer is not a simple one.

As believers, we are all explorers who seek to discover the truths contained in the Bible. We know that all truth is contained in the Word of God and that there really isn't any *new* truth to discover—after all, the Bible has been around for thousands of years—but some of the teachings we uncover will be new to *us*. That is why we can read the Bible over and over again and gain new insights every time. God's kingdom is vast, and there are many wonderful new things that we can discover each day.

A Rediscovery, Not a New Discovery

In the last century, a number of teachers and students of the Bible rediscovered and restored many important truths to the Body of Christ that had been lost, forgotten or submerged for centuries. Healing, worship, and the active involvement of the Holy Spirit's power in a believer's life are just a few of the truths that have experienced a renewed emphasis in the Church in recent decades.

However, every time God restores a truth to His Church, Satan attempts to plant an error. Usually, that error comes when someone begins to feel attacked or challenged on the "new" revelation that he or she has uncovered and then begins to carry a truth too far. This is what happened in the last century: Many of these teachers and students, in response to skeptics, critics and scoffers, began to reach too far. Some got carried away and began to abuse the truth that had been restored to the Church. Others in the Church seized on the abuse as an excuse to throw the baby out with the bathwater. Sadly, many people who would have benefited greatly by those truths ultimately rejected them.

Let me give you a silly, fictional parable that describes this phenomenon:

Back in the early days of this nation, an adventurer set out to explore the uncharted vastness of the North American continent. After many months of travel through forests and across immense prairies and deserts, he came across an enormous gorge—a huge hole in the earth.

Upon finding it, he thought to himself, *This big hole is spectacular. It's awe-inspiring! Other people should come here and see it*! So he went back home and began to tell others about the "Big Hole," as he had come to call it. He sent out advertisements and press releases on his discovery. But he couldn't get very many people interested in seeing it.

This frustrated him greatly. But one day, his wife said, "I think you have a marketing problem. The Big Hole doesn't really have much pizzazz as a name. What if you called it something more snazzy, like the 'Grand Canyon'?"

The man took his wife's advice, changed the name of the Big Hole to the Grand Canyon, and began to promote the majesty, glory and uniqueness of his discovery. In fact, to hear him tell it, he didn't just discover it—he practically invented it!

Well, more people soon began to visit the man's discovery. But with success came criticism. Some people questioned whether or not there really was a canyon there. Others admitted that it was there but it was terrifying rather than awe-inspiring. Many people believed that the man was wrong for trying to get people to go and see it.

This criticism wounded the man deeply. Offended and feeling rejected, he responded by making ever greater and more outlandish claims for his Grand Canyon. Soon, the Grand Canyon was all that he ever spoke about. He proclaimed it as the only natural wonder people ever needed to see in their lives. As a matter of fact, he became so centered on how great the Grand Canyon was that he stopped exploring altogether. He never traveled on to experience any of the other wonders that lay undiscovered in the West.

Meanwhile, others who heard his excessive claims (or who didn't like the man's intense style of communicating those claims) shrugged their shoulders and said, "I don't know about this Grand Canyon stuff. It's a little extreme. It's not for me." And thereby, they missed seeing one of the greatest natural wonders of the world.

I trust you picked up on the relevance of my little illustration. Yes, God wants us to prosper and do well. And yes, some people have taken this single truth to extremes and abused it. Similarly, some have taken the truth about the power of our words and stretched it farther than God's Word can support. They end up trying to get God to line up with their words instead of making sure their words line up with God!

Nevertheless, we must not miss the core truth that words have power. The Bible spends far too much time declaring this for us to dismiss it. For if we ignore this truth, we do so at our own peril.

Words—spoken and written—are clearly serious, powerful things to God.

In Scripture there is a wealth of wisdom and insight about the power of words, and together we're about to explore it. You can stop abusing the power of words—creating waste, hurt, lack and lifelessness. Instead, you're about to learn how to use that power to create wealth—spiritual, relational and material. Read on!

WORDS

CHAPTER ONE

The Strength in a Word

Remember, every time you open your mouth, your mind walks
out and parades up and down the words.
EDWIN H. STUART

There are about 800,000 words in the English language.[1] But 300,000 or so of these are technical words and scientific jargon used only by a narrow range of specialists in various fields and disciplines. That leaves you and me 500,000 words from which to select as we communicate in our daily lives.

Of course, nobody carries around a vocabulary of half-a-million words. In fact, the average person knows only about 10,000 words and uses only about 5,000 in everyday speech!

That's it—just 5,000 commonly used words to communicate a universe of ideas, emotions, events and desires. Yet, as you're about to see in the following pages, those words carry enormous power—the power to heal or wound; to encourage or dishearten; to speak truth or to deceive; to praise or to criticize.

I'm convinced that we don't think enough about our words and how much power they carry. That's why I've written this book. I want to reveal some amazing, neglected truths that can absolutely transform your life for the better. Indeed, I want to take you on a journey of discovery into more than just the obvious physical and emotional impact words can have. I want us to comprehend the magnitude of the spiritual force inherent in every word we speak.

I must tell you up front that it won't always be a comfortable journey. We'll travel through some territory that is likely to be painful to traverse. But if you stay with me, you'll find some keys to living more freely, more abundantly and more productively than you ever thought possible.

In a very real sense, this journey is a treasure hunt. Before we start, I need to let you know that the treasure map we'll be using is the Bible. Years of personal experience (and the uniform witness of thousands of others I have known) have persuaded me beyond all doubt that the Bible is God's infallible, reliable, living fountain of wisdom, revelation and truth. Those who drink deeply of it equip themselves to live an amazing life of achievement, influence and joy, and are able to become all that a loving God wants them to be. Former President Woodrow Wilson once said, "When you have read the Bible, you will know it is the Word of God, because you have found it the key to your own heart, your own happiness and your own duty."[2]

Now comes the painful part—for me. I'm going to tell you what my speech used to be like. Fortunately, my story has a happy ending.

A Loaded Gun

Has your tongue—what you say—ever gotten you in trouble? Mine certainly has. To be honest, for the first 20 to 25 years of my life, my tongue was my worst enemy. As a kid, it frequently got me beaten up. As an adolescent, it undermined my parents' trust in me and earned me frequent scrapes with the law. And in the early years of my marriage, it hurt my wife and weakened our relationship.

I grew up with a loaded gun for a mouth. Before I came to Christ, I abused the verbal gift God had put in me—the one that was designed to communicate His love and truth—and used it to manipulate and lie. I used what God had created as a tool for building people up to instead tear them down.

If someone hurt me or did something to embarrass me, that person was in for some serious payback. I meticulously planned my revenge—spending hours analyzing the person's weaknesses and vulnerabilities. Once I had formulated my plan, I would patiently wait for the perfect opportunity to humiliate that person in front of friends and classmates.

My warped thinking was, *I'm going to teach you to never come at me again.* And if anyone ever called me on it, my plea was, "Hey, I was just kidding. Just joking around. Something's wrong with you, not me."

I now know how very wrong and hurtful my behavior was. You can't say cutting remarks and then claim you didn't mean anything by them. (Unfortunately, I frequently see husbands and wives do that to each other.) The Bible says that you do mean something by what you say, because "out of the abundance of the heart the mouth speaks" (Matt. 12:34).

If my mouth was a loaded gun while I was growing up, over time I became highly skilled at pointing it at others and pulling the trigger. Not only could I embarrass a person, but I could also literally assault him or her with my words. This was not a good habit to bring into marriage.

I was not a Christian when Debbie and I got married, but I soon came to the knowledge of Christ as Savior. However, it was not until many months after our wedding that God got hold of me regarding the power of my words. In the years before I came to Christ, I had become a master of verbal manipulation. I could win any argument, even when I was dead wrong. And I carried all of these dark skills into our marriage. When, as most young married couples do, we had arguments, I instinctively put all of these skills to use. When we disagreed, I wasn't interested in finding agreement and harmony. I just wanted to win. And in order to win, I began to use my words to beat up on Debbie. I never laid a hand on her physically, but emotionally and verbally, I was a brute.

May I tell you something I have learned since those days of immaturity and insecurity? When you have manipulated and verbally bullied someone and he or she acquiesces simply because you are a more skillful debater—you have not won. In fact, you have lost—big time. My approach to relationships was costing me more than I could possibly imagine.

But all that changed one day. Nine months after our wedding day, Debbie and I were having an argument in which I, true to form, had twisted everything that she had said and had turned it against her to make her feel stupid. It was at this moment that God decided to get my attention.

My precious angel of a wife had just left the room in tears when I, a very young Christian who was just beginning to hear and recognize the voice of God, heard Him speak as clearly and firmly in my heart as I've ever experienced.

"You stop that."

"Excuse me, Lord?"

"Robert, do not ever do that again."

"C'mon Lord, I'm just blowing off a little steam. Everybody does it. It's healthy!"

Then, in the most serious tone of voice I've ever heard the Lord use, He said, *"You don't have the right to blow off steam at my daughter. You're hurting her. Stop it right now."*

My daughter?! The words stopped me in my self-assured tracks and made the hair on the back of my neck stand up. I suddenly saw everything I had been doing in a different light. Up to that moment, I had simply been arguing with "my" wife. Now I saw that what I was really doing was hurting God's beloved daughter. Even though I was a young Christian, I had enough holy fear of God to know that was something I didn't want to do. But God wasn't through adjusting my thinking.

"Do you remember that time you were beaten up by that karate black belt when you were a teenager?" He said. I thought for a moment, and then the memories came flooding back. My loud mouth and arrogant attitude had gotten me throttled on numerous occasions as I was growing up, but this one beating stood out from all the others. I was in a verbal altercation with a

certain guy who proceeded to warn me that he was a black belt in karate. Of course, my response was characteristically sarcastic and dismissive. I said, "I don't care what color your belt is!"

Well, I started caring a few minutes later. He gave me the beating of my life. I wasn't just sore for a few days, as I normally was after a fight. I was sore for weeks. In fact, I had bruised bones and muscles that were still tender months later.

God said to me, *"The reason it hurt for so long afterward is that he was skilled in combat. He knew what to do to hurt you."*

Then God dropped the bomb.

"Robert, you're like a black belt with your words. When you verbally beat up Debbie, it doesn't last just a little while. The hurt lasts a long time, because you're skillful with words. Stop doing that to my daughter. It's wrong, and you're going to ruin your marriage." God's words cut through my thick head and right to the quick of my heart.

That day was my wake-up call. I realized that I didn't need a devil working to destroy my life—me and my big mouth were doing a fine job of it all on our own. My mouth was making my life a wasteland. But when God stopped me in my tracks and I began to see certain truths in His Word and then apply those truths to my life with the help of the Holy Spirit, everything began to change for the better.

Allow me to show you a few of those basic truths that will form a foundation for everything else we explore. In later chapters, I'll be sharing some insights about the devastation that wrong words can bring as well as how our words can bring healing and restoration. But before we go there, let's take a look at *why* our words are so powerful.

Notes

1. *Oxford English Dictionary* (New York: Oxford University Press, 2005), n.p.
2. Woodrow Wilson, quoted at World of Quotes. http://www.worldofquotes.com/author/ Woodrow-Wilson:/1/index.html (accessed February 2006).

WORDS

CHAPTER TWO

Word Connections You Can't Live Without

Words have set whole nations in motion . . . Give me the right word and the right accent and I will move the world.

JOSEPH CONRAD

It was built in 1998 at a cost of $3.6 billion—the longest of its kind in the world. I'm referring to the Pearl Bridge, which connects Japan's main island of Honshu with the island of Shikoku. At a length of 6,470 feet (more than 2,300 feet longer than the Golden Gate Bridge in San Francisco), it's a marvel of modern engineering. It's also a powerful connector, spanning a deep-water barrier to unite two populations in meaningful and important ways.

But perhaps the greatest connector in engineering history was built nearly 100 years earlier. Prior to the completion of the Panama Canal in 1914, sailing from New York City to San Francisco meant a journey of 13,000 miles around the treacherous Cape Horn at the southern tip of South America. The canal lopped off 8,100 miles and much of the danger from that journey and connected the world of the Atlantic with the world of the Pacific, making the entire world a more accessible place.

Why the transportation history lesson in a book about words? Because there is something vital we need to understand about words.

Words are connectors.

Words have the capacity to build bridges, span chasms and shorten long distances between you and others. But words do not only connect you with other people—words also connect you with God.

Your God Connection

The Genesis account of creation shows how words were the vehicle God used in the spiritual realm to make things happen in the physical, or natural, realm. When God (who is spirit—see John 4:24) wanted something material created, He spoke.

In the opening lines of Genesis, we read, "Then God *said*, 'Let there be light'; and there was light" (Gen. 1:3, emphasis added). Over and over in the first three chapters of Genesis, as God is performing the astonishingly complex work of creating the universe, we see the words, "Then God *said.*"

God didn't wave His hand. He didn't bang a golden scepter on the ground. He spoke the material world into existence. In the first 25 verses of Genesis, God simply speaks, and things are. Then, in verses 26-27, we see God speak once more:

Then God said, "Let Us make man in Our image, according to
Our likeness; let them have dominion over the fish of the sea,

over the birds of the air, and over the cattle, over all the earth and over every creeping thing that creeps on the earth." *So God created man in His own image; in the image of God He created him; male and female He created them* (emphasis added).

We were created in God's image and likeness! Because God has creativity and the ability to create with His words, so do we. Of course, I'm not suggesting that the power we possess is even remotely like that of God's. But ever since God breathed into mankind His own breath of life, there's been a spark of what He is in us.

In Genesis 2:7, we get even more detail about the miracle of mankind's creation. It says that God "breathed into his nostrils the breath of life; and man became a living being" or "living soul." If you examine the Hebrew root words translated "living being" in that verse, you'll find that they can be literally rendered "speaking spirit."[1]

We're more than just dust-of-the-earth flesh. God has breathed spirit into us. We're not just physical beings; we have a spiritual component as well. We are speaking spirits.

We're the only species on Earth that can communicate our hearts, feelings, dreams, hopes and plans. Animals can send signals to one another that are understood at some level, but they can't communicate the deep things in their hearts (they have no spirit).

There's something creative and powerful about our speaking. That's why it's so important that we learn to control our tongues. They are loaded weapons that carry the very power to bring life or death to our relationships, our lives and our future.

Connecting with God Through Praise

When God needed to bridge the chasm of sin that separated us from Him, how did He connect with us? How did God get from the spiritual to the natural where we live? In the first chapter of John, we read:

In the beginning was the Word, and the Word was with God, and the Word was God . . . and the Word became flesh and dwelt among us (vv. 1,14).

The Word became flesh. The spiritual became natural. This very Word-bridge was prophesied in Psalm 107:20: "He sent His word and healed them, and delivered them from their destructions." God came to us through His Word—His Son, Jesus Christ. He is constantly bridging the gap with His Word. Thus, it shouldn't come as a surprise to learn that we are supposed to connect with God through our words.

Psalm 100 gives us clear instructions for coming into the presence of God. We're told to come into His presence with *singing*, to enter His gates with *thanksgiving*, to come into His courts with *praise*. Singing, thanksgiving and praise—all these actions are expressed through words.

The reason Satan doesn't want you to be vocal in your praise to God is because he knows that those kinds of words connect you to God in awesome ways. The simple truth is that the only people who experience the full glory and joy of God's presence are thankful people.

Satan will do everything he can to discourage you from expressing gratitude and praise. Frankly, he wants you to be a grumbler. Why? Because grumbling is an expression of unbelief and ingratitude (two big ways to short-circuit God's power in your life). Praise, on the other hand, is an expression of faith and gratitude.

Yes, words of praise are phenomenal connectors to God. But so are other types of words—such as prayer.

Any simple prayer offered from a sincere heart connects you to God. In Luke 18, Jesus illustrates a point by relating the parable of a woman praying day and night. After sharing this parable, Jesus drives home the point by saying, "Shall God not avenge His own elect who cry out day and night to Him?" (v. 7).

The idea of continual prayer is found in other Scripture as well. Ephesians 6:18 tells us to pray in the spirit "always." First Thessalonians 5:17 tells us to "pray without ceasing." Why do you think God wants us to pray day and night—always and without ceasing? Because He knows it keeps us connected to Him. Through praise and prayer it is possible to stay plugged in to God all day!

I'm not talking about striving to maintain your *position* in your relationship to God. If you're a Christian, then you're God's child. Your position in Him is steady and secure. He's faithful even when we are unfaithful (see 2 Tim. 2:13). I'm talking about having a connection to Him that allows you to hear His voice, feel His promptings, have access to His power and be anchored by His peace—even in the midst of the wildest storms of life. Don't you want that kind of connection to God—all day, every day?

Maybe you can think of a time—maybe it happened to you today—when a closer connection to God would have made all the difference. It's possible to have that kind of connection to Him through *praise* and *prayer*. That's why you will receive so much resistance from Satan when you use words to make a connection with God.

Fortunately for us, there are limits to what the devil can do. He cannot kill you just because he feels like it. (Believe me, if he had the power to kill you at any time, he would have already done it!) Let me tell you what he *can* do and will attempt to do on a continual basis throughout your life: He will try to deceive you so that you harm yourself; he'll try to sell you a lie that causes you to choose a self-destructive pattern of behavior; and, understanding the power of words as he does, he'll try to get you to turn your mouth against yourself.

When the serpent approached Eve in the garden to deceive her and break her connection to God, he chose words. He said to Eve, "Did God really say . . . ?" (Gen. 3:15, *NIV*). It's ironic, isn't it, that just as we use words to connect with God, Satan uses words to attempt to deceive us. He'll try to twist God's Word—to sow seeds of doubt in our minds about God's faithfulness, goodness or honor. He will do anything and everything he can to move us from gratitude to grumbling; from praise to self-pity. And, above all, he will try to discourage us from talking to God in prayer.

The key thing to remember, at all times, is that God bridges the gap to us through words, and we are to connect to Him in the same way. Here's a great passage of Scripture that shouts this principle. As you read it, note how many times you see the words "mouth," "word" and "call."

But what does it say? "The word is near you, even in your mouth and in your heart" (that is, the word of faith which we preach): that if you confess with your mouth the Lord Jesus and believe in your heart that God has raised Him from the dead, you will be saved. For with the heart one believes unto righteousness, and with the mouth confession is made unto salvation. . . . For "whoever calls on the name of the LORD shall be saved" (Rom. 10:8-13).

These verses have been the gateway to salvation for millions upon millions of people. How does a person get saved (get connected to God)? He walks the bridge of mouth-confession of the Lord Jesus Christ. He believes in his heart and he confesses with his mouth that Jesus Christ is Savior and Lord. As he does, he goes from the natural to the spiritual, from death to life, from hell to heaven.

What Disconnects Us from God

Here's the other side of this heart-mouth equation: Just as heart-belief and mouth-confession are the key elements in connecting a person to God, they are also the only thing that can permanently alienate a person from Him.

Let's look at a difficult and commonly misunderstood passage of Scripture. Jesus is speaking:

Therefore I say to you, every sin and blasphemy will be forgiven men, but the blasphemy against the Spirit will not be forgiven men. Anyone who speaks a word against the Son of Man, it will be forgiven him; but whoever speaks against the Holy Spirit, it will not be forgiven him, either in this age or in the age to come (Matt. 12:31-32).

I have counseled an astonishing number of people who were terrified that they had committed the unpardonable sin. It has been my pleasure to reassure them that the fact that they even care is ample evidence that they haven't committed the unpardonable sin. The reason so many people needlessly worry is that they don't continue reading after verse 32. When you read the entire chapter, you'll see that Jesus is speaking metaphorically about trees and fruit. He's likening the human heart to a tree, and the words of the mouth to the fruit that the tree produces.

That's why, immediately after warning His listeners (the Pharisees) about "the unpardonable sin," He says:

> Either make the tree good and its fruit good, or else make the tree bad and its fruit bad; for a tree is known by its fruit. Brood of vipers! How can you, being evil, speak good things? For out of the abundance of the heart the mouth speaks. A good man out of the good treasure of his heart brings forth good things, and an evil man out of the evil treasure brings forth evil things. But I say to you that for every idle word men may speak, they will give account of it in the day of judgment. For by your words you will be justified, and by your words you will be condemned (Matt. 12:33-37).

Jesus was talking about speaking against the Holy Spirit, and He pointed out that such speaking is evidence of an evil, unbelieving heart. In effect, He said to His audience, "Listen, if you've got a bad tree, you're going to have bad fruit. Your bad mouth is evidence of a bad heart." That's why the key sentence in that passage is "Out of the abundance of the heart, the mouth speaks."

What prompted this whole exchange with the Pharisees was Jesus doing what He always did—expressing God's highest will and desires for all of us by healing people and setting them free. The Pharisees observed this and from their hearts came this declaration: "This fellow does not cast out demons except by Beelzebub, the ruler of the demons" (Matt. 12:24). In other words, they claimed that Jesus' power came from Satan.

What kind of heart would produce that kind of declaration when the evidence showed people who had lived under the heel of dark demons all their lives now relishing the first joy and peace they had known in years?! People who had been blind from birth were seeing sunsets, flowers and the faces of their loved ones for the very first time. Crippled children who had never known the sensation of running through a field on a spring day were skipping and dancing as their parents wept for joy.

"He's of the devil" was the Pharisees explanation. Oh, what a dangerous thing it is to have a heart so cold, so hard, so twisted by pride, that you boldly declare that the good works of a holy God are authored by the destroyer and hater of mankind! And this is precisely what Jesus told them.

Jesus turned to the Pharisees and said, "Listen to me, guys. What you're doing right now could send you to hell. Let me tell you why. Your mouth is connected to your heart, and it is out of the abundance of your heart that your mouth is speaking right now. If you continue to have a heart like that, you'll never be able to receive God's grace, goodness and salvation. You will choose to go to hell instead."

What an important lesson for all of us! The words that come out of our mouths are a direct indicator of what is in our hearts.

Idle Words

There is, of course, another very sobering warning for all of us in Jesus' response to the blasphemous Pharisees:

> But I say to you that for every idle word men may speak, they will give account of it in the day of judgment. For by your words you will be justified, and by your words you will be condemned (Matt. 12:36-37).

"Every idle word"? I personally wish Jesus hadn't said that. But there it is.

Remember, we're discussing the value and the power of words. I don't know the exact value of a word, but I do know this: A word is worth so much that God is recording every single one of them for eternity. I don't know how He's doing it. I don't know if every person has an angel-scribe assigned to him or her. If so, I know some people who talk so fast and so much that their angel must surely be an expert in shorthand! I can just hear one angel in heaven saying to another, "Hey, please trade with me. I can't keep up with this guy anymore. I'm getting writer's cramp!"

I'm kidding of course. I don't believe that we actually have an angel assigned to us as a full-time recording secretary of our conversations. I believe that God personally remembers every word Himself! If you think that's too hard for Him, then you haven't studied enough about who He is. A God who spoke galaxies into existence and keeps the whole universe running as it should right down to the subatomic level wouldn't be mentally taxed at all to remember every single word from every single mouth on Earth—in this age or any other.

That's the bad news—every word you speak is being recorded. Now let me tell you the good news. Whatever kind of recording mechanism God used, it is equipped with an erase button. (I'm so glad that's the case, because I've said some pretty dumb things in my life.) Because of God's grace, when we confess our sins, including sins of the mouth, they are cleansed, erased and remembered no more! (See Psalm 103:3,12; 1 John 1:9.)

Nevertheless, we need to understand the importance of our words, because the Bible says that our works are going to be tried and tested:

> For no other foundation can anyone lay than that which is laid, which is Jesus Christ. Now if anyone builds on this foundation with gold, silver, precious stones, wood, hay, straw, each one's work will become manifest; for the Day will declare it, because it will be revealed by fire; and the fire will test each one's work, of what sort it is. If anyone's work which he has built on it endures, he will receive a reward. If anyone's work is burned, he will suffer loss; but he himself will be saved, yet so as through fire (1 Cor. 3:11-15).

What we do for God is going to one day stand as gold, silver and precious stones. But what we did in selfishness, pride, ambition or religiosity will be burned up. I suspect there are going to be a lot of believers surprised on the day of judgment when, though they are saved and heaven-bound, they find that much of what they did and said on Earth has been incinerated rather than rewarded.

Let me say once more that the unpardonable sin is not adultery—as hurtful and destructive as that is. It is not gambling. It's not even murder. It's the heart-mouth sin of a lifetime of prideful, unbelieving rejection of Jesus Christ.

The wonderful news is this: The same things that can give evidence of separation from God—words—can connect us to Him as well.

Your People Connection

Not only do words connect us to God, but in very important ways, words also connect us to each other. Words build bridges to strangers and keep existing relationships fresh. For good or ill, what we say determines the character and quality of those relationships. That's why Max De Pree, a member of *Fortune* magazine's National Business Hall of Fame, and a recipient of the Business Enterprise Trust's Lifetime Achievement Award, once said, "There may be no single thing more important in our efforts to achieve meaningful work and fulfilling relationships than to learn to practice the art of communication."[2]

Words are how we stay connected to each other. Nowhere is this more true or important than in marriage. To see an interesting validation of this truth, let's look at Proverbs 18:20-22:

> A man's stomach shall be satisfied from the fruit of his mouth, and from the produce of his lips he shall be filled. Death and life are in the power of the tongue, and those who love it will eat its fruit. He who finds a wife finds a good thing, and obtains favor from the LORD.

Allow me to paraphrase verses 20-21: "The quality of the life you are living depends on what you have been saying." In other words, your success, or lack thereof, depends a lot upon your mouth. I know people who have a belly full of bitterness, resentment, strife and broken relationships. Whether or not they know it, they're "eating" the fruit of their mouths. Conversely, others experience deep peace, blessings and the inward satisfaction that comes from harmonious relationships. It may seem odd, but in a very real spiritual sense, your mouth is producing the things that are filling your life.

I think it's significant that the verse that follows Proverbs 18:20-21 is a declaration about marriage. Why are these verses adjacent? I believe it is because your marriage will never be better than what proceeds from your mouth—it will never be better than what you build it to be from what you say. Stated another way, if you want to make a great marriage, you must make it with your mouth. If you want great kids, you must make them with your mouth. Life and death are in the power of the tongue. Far too many people spend a lot of time speaking death over their marriages.

Numerous studies have borne out this biblical truth. For example, when psychologists Cliff Notarius of Catholic University and Howard Markman of the University of Denver studied married couples during the first decade of marriage, they found a very subtle but important difference at the beginning of the relationships.

Among couples who ultimately stayed together, only 5 out of every 100 comments made about each other were putdowns. But among couples who later split up, 10 of every 100 (twice as many) comments were insults. That gap magnified over the following decade, until couples heading downhill were flinging five times as many cruel and belittling comments at each other as happy couples.

In their book based upon that research, Notarius and Markman wrote, "Hostile putdowns act as cancerous cells that, if unchecked, erode the relationship over time. In the end, relentless unremitting negativity takes control and the couple can't get through a week without major blowups."[3]

It's a sobering thought that the single most reliable predictor of success or failure in marriage wasn't how much affection a couple displayed, how many common interests they had, or what kind of economic background they sprang from. It was the kind of words they spoke to each other!

Stop speaking death to your spouse and start allowing your mouth to line up with the Word of God.

Husbands, begin praising your wife as if she already is the woman of God you want her to be. Stop tearing her down. Stop nit-picking. Quit making her the butt of your jokes with your friends. Ephesians 5:25-26 reads:

Husbands, love your wives, just as Christ also loved the church and gave Himself for it, that He might sanctify and cleanse it with the washing of water by the word.

Do you know how Jesus washes His wife (the Church)? According to this verse, it is with His words. So, husbands, are you washing your wife with your words? Are you cleansing her? Are you healing and restoring her? Are you encouraging her? Or is the opposite true as you discourage her, defile her and destroy her by your words. These are gravely serious questions to ask yourself.

The same issue applies to women. Wives, stop speaking death to your husband. Stop telling him all the things he does wrong. Find something—anything—he does right and praise him to the heavens for it. A lady once told a friend of mine that the only thing her husband did well was get out of bed. My friend's response was, "Then tell him he's the best getter-upper you've ever seen!" Encourage him! (If you want a good definition of the word "encourage," think of the word "courage." To *en*courage means "to put courage in." Conversely, to *dis*courage means "to draw courage out.")

Sometimes, when my wife, Debbie, and I go out to eat with a couple we've just met, we're shocked to hear how they tear each other down. It's truly astonishing. It's usually done in the guise of "just joking around." But let me tell you, it's not funny. It's destructive. And on most occasions, though there may be a forced smile on the face of the target, I see pain in the person's eyes. There is death in those insults.

I'm using marriage to show the connecting power of words, but these principles hold true for every relationship with another person. Your words can bring life or death to everyone you know. Think back on your past. Is there a severed relationship back there? If you think about how that came about, you'll probably see that words played a key role in the disconnection.

The good news is that the same instrument (words) that severed the relationship can also restore it. If you said something that hurt someone, the way to heal the breach is to say something else, namely, "I'm sorry. I was wrong. Please forgive me." By the way, those words are the most powerful and impacting words a child can ever hear a father say. For some reason, many men think that it's somehow weak or unwise to say "I'm sorry" to their kids. They fear that somehow they'll be surrendering their position of leadership and authority if they apologize.

Trust me, you won't. On the contrary, it's the best thing you can do if there's a disconnection between you and your children.

These words of confession are also the way you reconnect with God. If you're separated from God through disobedience or neglect, just use the connecting power of words to bring restoration: "If we confess [words!] our sins, He is faithful and just to forgive us our sins and to cleanse us from all unrighteousness" (1 John 1:9).

Raise the Standard

Stop speaking death over your health, your finances, your marriage and your other relationships. Start allowing your mouth to line up with the Word of God. Your words are either building bridges or blowing them up. It's one or the other, because words, more than anything else, connect us to God and to each other.

Over a period of years, I've learned that every time I raise the standard of the words I speak, my life gets better. I'm more effective in ministry and more successful as a husband, father and friend.

The same will be true for you. If you raise the standard for the words you speak to others, your marriage will get better. Your kids will do better. Your circumstances will improve.

You can determine your future quality of life by the words you speak today.

Notes
1. H. W. F. Gesenius, *Gesenius' Hebrew-Chaldee Lexicon to the Old Testament* (Grand Rapids, MI: Baker Book House 1984).
2. Max De Pree, *Called to Serve: Creating and Nurturing the Effective Volunteer Board* (Grand Rapids, MI: Wm. B. Eerdmans Publishing Company, 2001), n.p.
3. Clifford Notarius, Ph.D., and Howard Markman, Ph.D., *We Can Work It Out: How to Solve Conflicts, Save Your Marriage, and Strengthen Your Love for Each Other* (New York: Perigee Books; 1993), n.p.

WORDS

CHAPTER THREE

Can I Speak Freely?

*The real art of conversation is not only to say the
right thing in the right place, but to leave unsaid the
wrong thing at the tempting moment.*
DOROTHY NEVILL

Someone once came up to me after a church service and said, "Pastor,
your message kind of reminded me of the mercy of God. I thought it
would endure forever." (So much for tact and diplomacy.)

Winston Churchill was famous for bluntly saying pretty much whatever was on his mind, too. One such recorded comment was in response
to Lady Astor, who told him, "Sir, if you were my husband, I would poison
your drink." His reply was, "Madam, if you were my wife, I would drink it!"

"Can I speak freely?" is a familiar phrase in our culture. When a person says these words, he or she usually is seeking permission to set aside
tact and diplomacy and get brutally honest. (Now there's another interesting phrase; who wants to be brutalized by honesty?) In the words
"Can I speak freely?" I use the term "freely" in the sense of "at no cost."
But, is it possible to use words recklessly and indiscriminately without
them costing something?

In the previous chapter, we learned that Scripture says that words do indeed have tremendous value and power, with Jesus Himself giving a sobering warning about idle words (see Matt. 12:36).

So are any of our words "free"? Or is it possible that when we use our words wrongly or carelessly they can be turned around and used against us by the enemy? I want to point out three lies concerning words that Satan hopes every Christian will come to believe. Once those lies have been exposed, you will be in a much stronger position to avoid his deception and the damage it brings.

Lie #1: You Have the Right of Free Speech

I'm sorry to have to be the one to tell you this, but you do not have the right of free speech. Before you accuse me of being un-American, allow me to explain.

The First Amendment of the Constitution does guarantee every U.S. citizen the right of free speech (as well as freedom of religion, press and assembly.) And I'm so glad it does! I'm immensely grateful that I was born in a country in which the government is prohibited from telling me what I can and cannot say. Those freedoms were won and have been defended at enormous sacrifice. But even in the constitutional sense, there are limits to your right of free speech. Supreme Court Justice Oliver Wendell Holmes famously declared that our right to free speech doesn't give anyone the right to yell "Fire!" in a crowded theater.

Yes, I'm glad to be an American. But let me tell you something: When America has been gone for 100,000 years, heaven will still be here. Presidents come and go, but Jesus is still Lord—the same yesterday, today and forever (see Heb. 13:8).

We not only live under the laws of whatever country in which we were born, but we also are subject to spiritual laws—the unchanging principles that God has woven into the very fabric of creation. Every Christian carries a dual citizenship. In addition to our native countries, we're also citizens of the Kingdom of heaven. And as the laws of this Kingdom are concerned, there is no such thing as "free" speech. Words matter. They carry spiritual weight. And as we saw in the last chapter, we are ultimately accountable for how we use them.

Satan tries to get each of us to believe this isn't the case—that it doesn't really matter what we say and that we can say whatever we want with no consequences. He wants us to believe that words go out into the air and just disappear into vapor.

When I think about how deceived people can get about the cost of words and our accountability for the words we speak, shock-jock Howard Stern comes to mind. Stern is a 40-some-year-old man who has built a wildly successful radio career out of talking like a sex-obsessed 13-year-old boy. After repeatedly being fined by the Federal Communications Commission for violating decency standards, Stern recently announced that he was making the jump to satellite radio. Why? Because it is unregulated—giving him the freedom to be as vile and perverse as he wishes. In making the move, Stern claimed he was striking a blow for free speech. (He apparently was also striking a blow for free enterprise. His deal with Sirius satellite radio will pay him $500 million over a five-year period.)

Stern moved to satellite radio because he didn't want to have to be accountable for the words he speaks. But I have news for him. His words are being recorded by an Authority much higher than the FCC. And like the rest of us, he will one day stand before a Judge of unimaginable power, glory and holiness. There he'll be ordered to give an account for every word not covered by the blood of Christ.

For some people, the realization that there is no such thing as free speech will come too late.

You simply cannot say anything you want. Believer or unbeliever, you are going to be held accountable for every word you say. Once you realize that fact, it's easy to see why the psalmist wrote:

Set a guard, O LORD, over my mouth;
Keep watch over the door of my lips (Ps. 141:3).

That would be good Scripture to memorize and put on your bathroom mirror. In fact, we would all be well served to say that verse as a prayer first thing every morning.

It is important to remember that anytime you feel the need to begin a conversation with the words, "I probably shouldn't tell you this, but . . ." it's almost always a conversation that shouldn't happen at all. So, if you feel the need to say, "I probably shouldn't say this . . ." then DON'T! Just hush. That little nudge you are feeling is probably the Holy Spirit saying, "Don't go there. You're going to regret the words you're about to speak." Or as King David wrote, "Muzzle it!"

> I said, "I will guard my ways, lest I sin with my tongue; I will restrain my mouth with a muzzle" (Ps. 39:1).

Oh, yes, you can sin with your tongue! David knew this and took special steps to keep himself from that kind of sin. He knew how serious God is about the damage and destruction the tongue can do. He obviously passed this knowledge along to his son, Solomon, because in Proverbs 6, Solomon wrote:

> These six things the LORD hates,
> Yes, seven are an abomination to Him:
> A proud look,
> A lying tongue,
> Hands that shed innocent blood,
> A heart that devises wicked plans,
> Feet that are swift in running to evil,
> A false witness who speaks lies,
> And one who sows discord among brethren (vv. 16-19).

"Hate" and "abomination" are strong words. And in this list of seven things that are an abomination to God, three of them are sins of the mouth.

Free speech? Don't believe the lie. There's nothing free about it.

Lie #2: If You're "Just Kidding," It Doesn't Count

"Hey, I was just kidding!"

"What's the matter? Can't you take a joke?"

"Hey, I was joking! Come on, where's your sense of humor?"

"Gee, you're so sensitive."

These are phrases commonly used by people who are trying to get off the hook after saying something mean, insensitive, manipulative or insulting. I know, because I used them all.

For many years, I bought in to the lie that as long as I was "just kidding," it didn't matter what I said. This is not a new deception. It was obviously prevalent 3,000 years ago, because in Proverbs 26, we read:

> Like a madman who throws firebrands, arrows, and death, is the man who deceives his neighbor, and says, "I was only joking!" (vv. 18-19).

To use words recklessly or dishonestly and then appeal to the I-was-just-kidding defense is like throwing red-hot iron, shooting arrows and flinging death at others!

Imagine if someone you knew burst into your home with a deer-hunting bow and fired an arrow at you, striking you in the leg. You'd probably say, "Hey, what on earth are you doing? You wounded me! Are you nuts?! You could have killed me!" What would you think if that acquaintance replied, "Hey, it's a joke! C'mon, where's your sense of humor?"

Hurtful words pierce people and go deep into their souls. You can't get out of it by saying you were just joking.

When I think of the years that my mouth shot out hurtful words, I am forever grateful that God stopped me and that I began to study His thoughts about the power of words.

We must utterly reject the lie that we can say what we want as long as we offer the "just kidding" defense later.

Lie #3: Once Your Words Are Forgotten, Their Influence Is Gone

It is very easy for Satan to persuade us that as soon as our words are forgotten, their influence is gone—that once someone has forgotten what you said, it doesn't affect or influence him or her anymore. This thinking represents one of the most widely believed lies about words.

Words echo through eternity and have lasting repercussions.

Jesus said that you and I are going to have to give an account for the words we speak. Satan, the father of lies, tells us just the opposite—that words evaporate. They just go out into the air and dissolve into nothingness.

We read in James 3:5-6 that "even so the tongue is a little member and boasts great things. See how great a forest a little fire kindles! And the tongue is a fire."

I've started more than my share of conflagrations with this Zippo®-lighter tongue of mine. Before I was saved, I set off some blazes that would make the Great Chicago Fire look like a weenie roast.

How about you? Have you ever made a thoughtless, careless comment and then later marveled at the damage it caused? It's easy to do. Our homes, workplaces and churches are tinderbox-dry forests that are easily set ablaze.

What we often do after we say something hateful or mean is give the person we've just verbally singed with our fiery words the feeling that they should just get over it—just move on and not make such a big deal out of it. (Easy to say but virtually impossible to do.)

To my deep sorrow and regret, my words took a toll on the person I love most on this earth. I've already mentioned how, in the early years of my marriage, I twisted and manipulated words in arguments with my wife, Debbie, to the point that I was hauled up short by God Himself. Deeply repentant and filled with genuine remorse, I asked Debbie's forgiveness and threw myself upon God's throne of grace for help. And help me, He did.

If you ask Debbie, she will testify that things were markedly different from that day forward. I was far from perfect. I still slipped from time to time. But a stronghold in my life was broken that night.

Words That Heal

Bad words last, but good words last longer. Let me tell you a story I read awhile back that expresses this truth so well.

Many years ago, a seminary professor was vacationing with his wife in Gatlinburg, Tennessee. One morning, they were eating breakfast at a little restaurant, hoping to enjoy a quiet family meal. While they were waiting for their food, they noticed a distinguished-looking, white-haired man moving from table to table, chatting with the guests. The professor leaned over and whispered to his wife, "I hope he doesn't come over here." But sure enough the man eventually did amble over to their table.

"Where are you folks from?" he asked in a friendly voice.

"Oklahoma," they answered.

"Great to have you here in Tennessee," the white-haired stranger said. "What do you do for a living?"

"I teach at a seminary," the professor replied.

"Oh, so you teach preachers how to preach, do you? Well I've got a really great story for you." And with that the gentleman, uninvited, pulled up a chair and sat down at the table with the couple. The professor groaned and thought to himself, *Great. Just what I need—another cheesy sermon illustration. I bet I've already heard it.*

The old gentleman pointed out the restaurant window and said, "Do you see that mountain over there? Not far from the base of that mountain there was a boy born to a poor unwed mother. He had a very hard time of it growing up, because every place he went he was always asked the same question. "Hey boy, who is your daddy?"

The identity of the illegitimate child's father was a mystery the town gossips were constantly trying to solve. So, whether he was at school or at the grocery store, people would ask him the same question— "Who's your daddy, son?" Sometimes the question came innocently from a stranger. But usually it was asked out of meanness and spite. Regardless, he heard that question wherever he went. And he dreaded it.

He would hide at recess and lunch time from other students. Many times he would avoid going out in public because those words hurt him so badly. On Sundays, the boy would always go to church late and slip out early in order to avoid the disapproving stares and the dreaded question.

Then, when he was about 12 years old, a new pastor was assigned to his church. And on that day, the pastor finished the benediction so quickly that the boy got caught and had to walk out with the crowd. Just about the time he got to the back door, the preacher saw the unaccompanied child, put his hand on his shoulder and said, "Hi there, son. Who is your daddy?"

A sudden hush fell over the exiting crowd. The boy felt his face flush as he sensed every eye in the church looking at him. How would he answer? Now everyone would finally know the answer to the question. The mystery would be solved.

This new pastor instantly sensed the awkwardness of the situation and, following a prompting from the Holy Spirit, quickly followed his question with these words:

"Wait a minute," he said, "I know who you are. I see the family resemblance now. You are a child of God." With that he took hold of the boy's shoulders, looked him square in the eye and said, "Son, you have a great inheritance. Go and claim it."

A smile bigger than anyone had ever seen flashed across the boy's face. And he walked out the church door a changed person because of the words that were spoken to him that day. From that day forward, whenever anybody asked him about his daddy, he just told them, "I'm a child of God."

The distinguished gentleman got up from the table and said, "Isn't that a great story?"

Touched by the story, the professor admitted, "Yes, it really is a great story."

As the old man walked away, he turned and offered one final comment. "You know, if that new pastor hadn't told me that I was one of God's children, I probably never would have amounted to anything." And then he walked away.

The seminary professor and his wife were stunned and deeply moved to learn that the man had been speaking of himself. They called the waitress over and asked, "Do you know that older gentleman who just left our table? Who is he?"

The waitress grinned and said, "Of course. Everybody knows him. That's Ben Hooper, the former governor of Tennessee."[1]

. . . .

The power of words! What that pastor spoke to the little boy who would eventually become a state governor changed his life.

Here's the truth about words, straight from Scripture: We do not have the right to speak "freely" at all times; we cannot claim that we were "just kidding" when we break hearts and spirits with our words; and we are deceived if we believe that our negative words evaporate into thin air and are quickly forgotten.

But positive words can bring healing, and they have a shelf life with no expiration date.

Words—good or bad—last forever.

Note

1. Ben W. Hooper and Everett R. Boyce, *The Unwanted Boy: The Autobiography of Governor Ben W. Hooper* (Knoxville, TN: University of Tennessee Press, 1963), n.p.

CHAPTER FOUR

Ten Deadly Sins of the Tongue

Normally when we think about the evil things men do,
we think about those who drink alcohol, those who steal, those who are
involved in some form of immorality, those who
murder, those who are violent and abuse others physically.
But how often do we think about all the evil that is done through the
use, or misuse, of the tongue?

AL MACIAS

If you grew up Catholic or Episcopalian, you can probably recite the Seven Deadly Sins (pride, envy, gluttony, lust, anger, greed, sloth). If you have a Baptist or evangelical background, you may not be able to name all seven without some help, but you've certainly heard of the list. (By the way, in the church where I grew up, the list was even longer than seven items!)

Likewise, many people are familiar with the first two verses of Isaiah 59, but they've never heard (or read) the third verse (italicized below):

Behold, the LORD's hand is not shortened, that it cannot save; nor His ear heavy, that it cannot hear. But your iniquities have separated you from your God; and your sins have hidden His face from you, so that He will not hear. *For your hands are defiled with blood, and your fingers with iniquity; your lips have spoken lies, your tongue has muttered perversity.*

Here's my paraphrase of this passage: "God hasn't stopped hearing you and He is certainly powerful enough to help you. That's not your problem. You're experiencing all this trouble because your sins have separated you from God's power and blessing. Here's a list of those sins!"

Verse 3 is a serious list of offenses. Notice that right beside "hands defiled with blood"—in other words, "murder"—we see lips that "have spoken lies" and tongues that have "muttered perversity." In other words, there are sins of the hands and sins of the tongue. Both have the effect of severing our connection to God's delivering power.

Please don't misunderstand. This passage isn't speaking of being separated from salvation; our salvation is by grace through faith in Jesus Christ. Verse 3 is about how our sins affect our intimacy with God and our ability to overcome trouble and tribulation in the here and now.

Let me give you an example. As believers, we are, in a very real sense, married to God. When we come into this relationship, we become a part of the bride of Christ (see John 3:29; Rev. 18:23; 21:9). If you were continually lying to your spouse, would it affect your intimacy? Of course it would; but it probably wouldn't result in divorce. When we lie, our relationship with God is also affected, but He has promised us, "I will never leave you nor forsake you" (Heb. 13:5). God is not going to divorce us because of our sin, but sin certainly does affect our closeness to Him.

Here, then, is what Isaiah 59:3 is saying: If you find yourself separated from God, there is nothing wrong on His part. The reason you're not getting your prayers answered is because the sins of your hands or the sins of your mouth have separated you from God.

Most of us are much more likely to be guilty of sins of the mouth. When we commit such sins, we're saying things that don't line up with the Word of God. We are telling God that He can't trust us. He hears our prayers, but He can't answer them because the way our mouths operate every day does not line up with our prayers or with His Word.

Ten Symptoms of a Sick Tongue

The previous three chapters have shown us that it is possible to sin with our mouths. In fact, the sins of the mouth can be grouped into 10 basic categories. Borrowing from the traditional label, I call these categories "The Ten Deadly Sins of the Tongue," because when we commit these sins, we are actually speaking death.

I know this isn't fun news, but please stay with me. We'll be getting to the good news soon! But before we can write a prescription for an illness, that illness has to be accurately diagnosed. That's why I want to take you through these 10 possible symptoms of a sick tongue. As you read, see how many of them may apply to you.

Symptom #1 – Telling the *Untruth*

Every person on planet Earth above the age of three knows that it is wrong to lie. Yet lying may be the most widespread and common of all human activities. The ancient Greek philosopher, Diogenes, is said to have traveled all over Athens carrying a lantern in daylight—searching, in vain, for an honest man.

Lying may be common, but that doesn't mean God approves of it. In fact, as we learned in the previous chapter, Bible makes it clear that God hates it:

These six things the LORD hates, yes, seven are an abomination to Him: a proud look, a lying tongue, hands that shed innocent blood, a heart that devises wicked plans, feet that are swift in running to evil, a false witness who speaks lies, and one who sows discord among brethren (Prov. 6:16-19).

Notice again that of the seven things listed that God hates, three have to do with the mouth. Two of them relate to lying. And they are an "abomination" to Him. That's a very strong term, and it's not the last time the term is used to describe God's feelings about lying. In Proverbs 12:22, we find that "lying lips are an abomination to the LORD, but those who deal truthfully are His delight."

In the original text of the Bible, there are several Hebrew and Greek words that are translated into the English word "sin." The word most frequently used is the Greek word *hamartano*, which means "to miss the mark." Perhaps you've heard a preacher define sin as simply missing the mark on a target. This is the word translated "sin" in the well-known verse, "For all have sinned and fall short of the glory of God" (Rom. 3:23).

There are, however, some words that convey a much stronger sense than merely missing the mark. Such is the Hebrew word translated "abomination" in Proverbs 6:16 (*to`ebah*). This word refers to something that is utterly detestable. It is something disgusting. It is the Hebrew word used most frequently to describe God's feeling about His people worshiping pagan idols. And this is precisely the word used to describe God's attitude toward lying.

Lying is abominable and detestable to God. Why? Because it is the antithesis of who He is. God is truth. He doesn't just *have* truth, He *is* truth. At the other end of the spectrum, the Bible describes Satan as "the father of lies" (John 8:44, *NIV*).

Thus, when we lie, we leave the throne of God and go to the throne of Satan. No wonder God views lying as detestable!

Lying is a subject I know a lot about. You see, before I came to Christ, I was a chronic and skillful liar. There is no other way to say it.

I remember the first time I got caught in a bold-faced lie. I was about eight years old. My father had left some money on the kitchen counter, and I helped myself to it. My father knew that I had taken it, but he was going to give me the opportunity to show some character and come clean.

So he asked me, "Robert, where is the money that was on the counter?"

"I don't know," I replied, knowing that it was in the pocket of my jeans.

"Did you take it, son? Did you pick it up accidentally?"

"No."

Giving me every chance in the world to tell him the truth, he said, "Well, we're going to turn the house upside down until we find that money. We are not going to stop looking for it until we find it." He knew that I was beginning down a road that didn't lead to a good place.

We began to search, and from time to time I'd say, "Dad, it's just not here. It has just disappeared. It's just not in the house." And he would reply, "It *is* in the house, and we're going to find it."

When I realized he wasn't going to give up, I knew I had to do something. So I slipped the money out of my pocket, dropped it behind a chair in the living room and then pretended to "discover" it.

"Hey, I found it! Here it is!"

"Son, you put it there," my father said with sadness and weariness in his voice.

"No, I didn't." I compounded one lie upon another. That was my way.

Finally, I admitted the truth, and my dad took me to a private room to discipline me. My father never disciplined me inappropriately. He was not a violent man. He spanked me and did it the Bible way—in love and sorrow, not in anger; as correction, not retribution.

After he spanked me, he did something he'd never done before. He said, "I just spanked you for stealing. Now I am going to spank you for lying." He paddled me again.

My father handled everything in that situation correctly. But even at that early age, my mind was so corrupt that the moment he left the room demons began to talk to me. My immediate thoughts were not along the lines of Boy, *I'll never do that again. I have really learned my lesson.* On the contrary, my first thought was, *I don't ever want to get caught again. I need to get better at lying.*

So from that point forward, I began to rehearse my stories and think through all the possibilities in advance. In other words, I got good at lying. I developed lying into an art form. And it became a habit in my life. In scriptural language, it became a "stronghold" in my life—a deeply ingrained, demonically reinforced habit. Lying certainly had a strong hold on me.

Nine months after Debbie and I were married, I surrendered my life to Christ. But lifetime habits and strongholds do not evaporate the moment you get saved. (I've heard of some cases where that has happened, but it's not the norm.) Romans 12:2 tells us that, as believers, transformation comes as we renew our minds. In other words, transformation is a process.

As a newlywed and a new Christian, I was still very much in the habit of lying as a lifestyle. Nevertheless, it wasn't long after my salvation experience that I began preaching.

Believe it or not, I would find myself in the middle of a sermon, and I would tell a lie! Some would call it poetic license, but God calls it lying. I was exaggerating (and occasionally fabricating) for the sake of emphasis and impact. My rationalization was that is was for a good cause! The truth is, lying had become so integrated into my communication style that it just came naturally.

Of course, the Lord began to convict me. He'd say to me, "You're still lying." And I'd reply, "You're right, Lord. I'll never do it again." I meant what I told Him, but following through was a different matter. On the heels of my declaration never to lie again would come a lie. This happened time and again.

How does one break a cycle of defeat like this?

Please pay close attention, because this principle applies to overcoming all 10 of the deadly sins of the tongue. Here is the twofold key to breaking a stronghold.

You become *accountable* and *correctable*.

You give key people a view to your pattern of behavior *and* the permission to correct you when they see you engaging in it. This means giving people permission to speak into your life and to hold you accountable. The person I needed to tell about my pattern of lying and then give the permission to keep me accountable was Debbie.

When I finally got this revelation, I went to Debbie and said, "I don't know if you know this or not, but I have a problem with lying." She said, " Oh, I know." (Of course, she knew!)

"Well, I want you to correct me," I said. "If you hear me tell a lie or stretch the truth, I want you come to me privately and call me on it."

After some initial trepidation, she agreed.

From then on, we would get in the car after I had preached a sermon and she would so gently and tactfully say to me, "Honey, I hate to bring this up, but I noticed you exaggerated a little tonight."

"Really?" I would say. "No way!"

"Well, sweetheart, actually, you did."

"Are you sure? When?"

"Well, do you remember that part where you said 200 people got saved at the revival you preached last weekend? Well, it was actually 7. Remember?"

It wasn't long before the accountability that Debbie provided, along with lots of prayer, began to break down that stronghold. Soon, I would find myself preaching a sermon and right in the middle of an illustration, I would pause. I would catch myself about to enhance the story for effect and then would think, "Debbie is going to call me on this when we get in the car. I'd better stick with the truth."

Do you see how accountability and correction can work together? Give your spouse, your friend, or a pastor permission to correct you. It's the key to overcoming all the deadly sins of the tongue, including the first one—lying.

Symptom #2 – Stirring Up Division

Let's consider the words "one who sows discord among brethren" (Prov. 6:19) in context with the verses that come before it.

> A worthless person, a wicked man, walks with a perverse mouth; he winks with his eyes, he shuffles his feet, he points with his fingers; perversity is in his heart, he devises evil continually, *he sows discord.* Therefore his calamity shall come suddenly; suddenly he shall be broken without remedy (Prov. 6:12-15, emphasis added).

Notice the specific reason why this "worthless person" is going to experience sudden calamity and brokenness without remedy: "He sows discord."

What a serious thing it is to stir up strife, especially among Christian brothers and sisters. That's why I'm so grieved whenever I see someone stirring up strife in the church. I fear for that person's well-being, because the Word says that calamity will come on him suddenly.

I hate to be the one to tell you this, but if you are a person who goes around sowing discord, calamity is on its way to your house. Such warnings are not limited to the Old Testament:

> But avoid foolish disputes, genealogies, contentions, and strivings about the law; for they are unprofitable and useless. Reject a divisive man after the first and second admonition, knowing that such a person is warped and sinning, being self-condemned (Titus 3:9-11).

Let me tell you how devious the enemy is. Satan is so insidiously stealthy about the sins of the mouth that he has convinced some people that they're actually doing good by bringing up things they shouldn't be bringing up. He has convinced some that they are guardians of the truth. So they run from person to person, relating what the other person said. "I just thought you should know . . ." is the common rationalization.

In actuality, such people are being used by Satan to sow discord in the church. Scripture says they bring sudden calamity upon themselves. It is an extremely serious thing to sow discord among brethren.

The Baptist preacher A. B. Simpson surely had this in mind when he said, "I would rather play with forked lightning, or take in my hand living wires with their fiery current, than speak a reckless word against any servant of Christ, or idly repeat the slanderous darts which thousands of Christians are hurling on others, to the hurt of their own souls and bodies."[1]

Be a peacemaker rather than a troublemaker. God is a reconciler, and we should emulate Him. God sent His Son into the world for one reason—to reconcile all mankind to Himself. That's why He hates discord so much. He paid a terrible price to bring people together. He doesn't look kindly on any activity that drives them apart.

Be super-vigilant if someone comes to you and opens up about his or her marriage. Be sure that, in an attempt to comfort or show support, you don't sow discord in that marriage. Be very aware of the effect your words will have.

A biblical response in this type of situation would be to say, "It may be hard right now, but you need to honor your husband." Or, "It may not come easy, but you need to love your wife and treat her like a queen." Don't you dare get caught up in the emotion of your friend's hurt and get offended on his or her behalf and start agreeing with what your friend is saying about how insensitive, selfish or irrational his or her spouse is.

If you sow discord in a marriage, you are getting in trouble with God. So bring people together. Don't be a part of driving them apart.

Symptom #3 - Dishing the Dirt

Around the time of the First World War, Morgan Blake, a sportswriter for the *Atlanta Journal* newspaper, wrote:

> I am more deadly than the screaming shell from the howitzer. I win without killing. I tear down homes, break hearts, and wreck lives. I travel on the wings of the wind. No innocence is strong enough to intimidate me, no purity pure enough to daunt me. I have no regard for truth, no respect for justice, no mercy for the defenseless. My victims are as numerous as the sands of the sea, and often as innocent. I never forget and seldom forgive. My name is Gossip.[2]

A gossip is a person who habitually spreads intimate or private rumors or facts. Notice that I included the term "facts." Some people claim that it's not gossip if it's the truth. They are deceiving themselves. True or not, it's gossip if it's private or intimate in nature.

From God's viewpoint, if you are not part of the problem or essential to the solution, there is no reason to talk about a private matter. He says so repeatedly in His Word: "A gossip betrays a confidence; so avoid a man who talks too much (Prov. 20:19, *NIV*). That's pretty clear, isn't it? So is, "A troublemaker plants seeds of strife; gossip separates the best of friends" (Prov. 16:28, *NLT*). I suspect you could testify to the truth of that Scripture.

And then there is this passage from Paul to the church at Corinth:

For I am afraid that when I come to visit you I won't like what I find, and then you won't like my response. I am afraid that I will find quarreling, jealousy, outbursts of anger, selfishness, backstabbing, gossip, conceit, and disorderly behavior (2 Cor. 12:20, *NLT*).

Clearly, gossip in the Church is not a new problem. It's as old as the Church itself. I suspect they disguised it back then the same way we do today, by saying, "I'm only telling you this so that you can pray about it." Right.

Here's a great way to test yourself the next time you're about to use the I'm-telling-you-this-so-you-can-pray-about-it rationalization. Before you tell your juicy story, ask yourself, "Am I praying about it?" Then be gut-level honest with God in your answer. If you haven't spent significant time on your knees in fervent intercession over the situation, you're just gossiping. And it's wrong. What's more, it's deadly.

Are you burdened about it? Does it break your heart? Are you lifting the situation to the Father's throne of grace? Have you talked to God about it more than you have talked to others about it? If not, it's gossip.

If you're still not sure if you're tempted to gossip, ask yourself: Do I get excited when I hear the words, "Have you heard . . .?" Do my ears perk up? Is there a part of me that enjoys hearing "dirt" on a fellow believer? If so, you know the answer—it's gossip.

Like other sins of the tongue, gossip is a habit. If this a problem for you, then it is a stronghold and it's separating you from God. It's robbing you of your intimacy with Him. And it will cut you off from God's delivering power and His blessing.

Sometimes you need to say gently but firmly to someone who is about to tell you juicy news, "Do I really need to hear this?"

I've learned to do this myself. I'll say, "I'm sure you're burdened about that situation, and I'm confident that you're praying about it; but I really don't need to hear the details. I'll just let the Holy Spirit guide me in prayer about it. He knows what will help the situation." (By the way, this is another important role of "praying in the Spirit." I'll share more about that in a later chapter.)

Break the gossip habit. Tear down that stronghold. It's a deadly sin of the tongue.

Symptom #4 – Passing Along False Information

Slander is closely related to gossip. In fact, they often walk hand in hand. Slander is a false and malicious statement or report about someone.

You may be saying, "I would never do that!" But did you know that many times we unknowingly slander someone when we pass along negative information we've heard but don't know for sure that it's true? I bet you've done that. I know I have.

When we say to someone, "Did you hear that so and so did such and such?" we often find out later that we heard wrong or incomplete information. Or we're passing on an outright lie initiated by someone with evil intent.

In such a situation, you may be tempted to justify what you've done: "I'm innocent because I was given bad information!" But you're not innocent. If you had applied the "gossip test" I described above, you would have never said anything in the first place. And in saying something, you became guilty of the sin of slander. How does God view this practice?

> Let not a slanderer be established in the earth; let evil hunt the violent man to overthrow him (Ps. 140:11).

> Whoever spreads slander is a fool (Prov. 10:18, *NIV*).

Slander is clearly something you don't want to be involved in; and according to God's Word, you don't want to associate with someone who commits slander!

> But now I am writing you that you must not associate with anyone who calls himself a brother but is sexually immoral or greedy, an idolater or a slanderer, a drunkard or a swindler. With such a man do not even eat (1 Cor. 5:11, *NIV*).

This doesn't mean that if someone has momentarily fallen into sin that you can't have a relationship with him. Paul is telling the church at Corinth (and us), "You must not let such a person continue to be a member in good standing in your church. You have confronted him and begged him with a loving attitude to repent, but he is persistent in that lifestyle. You cannot wink at that man's sin. It will destroy the church." This is talking about a lifestyle of someone who flagrantly and unrepentantly walks in sin. Slander is one of the sins mentioned alongside such serious offenses as sexual immorality, idolatry and swindling.

George Sweeting, the former president of Moody Bible Institute, once said, "There's only one thing as difficult as unscrambling an egg, and that's unspreading a rumor.[3]

Slander is serious. And sadly, it is far too common, even among God's people.

Symptom #5 – Breaking Confidences

The fifth deadly sin of the tongue is what the Bible, in King James English, calls talebearing. It refers to the act of revealing secrets or breaking a confidence. It is mentioned in Proverbs 11:13:

> A talebearer reveals secrets, but he who is of a faithful spirit conceals a matter.

Sometimes you can discover what something *is* by learning about its opposite. That's the case with this proverb. It describes the opposite of a talebearer so that you can better understand what a talebearer is. What is the opposite of a talebearer? A "faithful" person who "conceals a matter."

If there is any place where you should be safe to confess your sins, it should be among the Body of Christ. If there is any place that you should be able to get help when you need it, it should be the Church. People should be able to come to us and tell us their deepest and darkest secrets, and they should be safe with us. But that isn't always the case.

I'm not talking here about being a party to concealing illegal, dangerous or hurtful activity. If someone came to me with information about child abuse or a potential suicide attempt, I wouldn't keep that a secret.

I'm talking about someone saying, "I have a problem in this area." Doing so, by the way, is quite biblical. James says, "Confess your faults one to another, and pray for one another, that ye may be healed" (Jas. 5:16, *KJV*).

With that in mind, let me ask you: Is it possible that there are a lot of people in the Church who are not healed—emotionally, spiritually or even physically—because they won't confess their faults to one another? And is it possible that many won't confess their faults to one another because they have done so in the past and been burned by talebearers who spread their embarrassing weaknesses and failures all over the church? We have to become, as in the verse in Proverbs, faithful spirits who know how to conceal a matter.

This reminds me of a practice I've never understood. Have you ever shared a confidential matter with someone only to have it get back to you through the grapevine? When you confronted the person in whom you confided, she probably said, "Well, I told so-and-so, but she promised not to tell anyone!" And guess what? So-and-so demanded the same promise from the person she told, and so on.

Listen, when you tell someone something that you're supposed to be keeping a secret, and you ask him to promise not to tell anyone, what you're doing is hoping that he is more honorable and trustworthy than you are!

When someone shares something with you and you agree not to share it with anyone else, do you know what that means? (This is profound, so you don't want to miss it.) It means that you don't share it with anyone else!

Yet we blab confidential information all the time. Why? Because there is a carnal part inside all of us that enjoys showing others that we are privy to secret information. We enjoy dishing out tasty tidbits—which is just what Proverbs 18:8 is talking about when it says:

> The words of a whisperer [talebearer] are like dainty morsels,
> and they go down into the innermost parts of the body (*NASB*).

It is absolutely essential that we become a safe place for people to share faults, failures and weaknesses. When someone confesses something to you, he is giving you power. He is entrusting some power over his life to you. Now let me tell you what character is. It is having power and handling it wisely. That is the best definition of character I know.

Don't break a confidence. Talebearing is a deadly sin of the tongue.

Symptom #6 – Speaking Curses Instead of Blessings

Today the verb "cursing" has come to mean "using profane language." In fact, in my native Texas, the word has morphed over the decades into the slang word "cussing," as in, "After he dropped that bowling ball on his foot, he was cussing up a storm." However, when the Bible uses the word "cursing," it has a much broader and more significant meaning than simply using bad language.

Look, for example, at Romans 3:13-14:

> Their throat is an open tomb; with their tongues they have practiced deceit; the poison of asps is under their lips; whose mouth is full of cursing and bitterness.

Here Paul is describing a group of people who have a serious problem with their words. Look at that list:

- Throats that are an open tomb—in other words, they are filled with death and decay.
- Tongues that have practiced deceit—in other words, they are skilled in lying.
- Lips with the poison of asps under them—in other words, they are concealing snake venom.
- Mouths that are filled with "cursing and bitterness."

This is obviously not a pretty picture. But just what is cursing? In the Bible, cursing refers to the act of pronouncing a curse upon someone.

Cartoons and Hollywood movies have ingrained the impression that pronouncing curses is something only old gypsy women and tribal witch doctors do. But if you read your Bible, you'll discover that everyone who has a voice has the power to do two important things with it: bless or curse. In fact, cursing is the exact opposite of blessing. As every page of this book has reinforced—our words have power and consequences!

Jesus understood the power of cursing. Remember when He and the disciples approached a fig tree? The tree, by being green and leafy, advertised that it had fruit. But when Jesus and His disciples got close, they saw that it had no fruit. That's when Jesus said these words to the tree: "Let no one eat fruit from you ever again" (Mark 11:14).

Of course, when they came back by that tree the next day, they found it withered from the roots up. The disciples marveled, but Jesus wasn't surprised at all. Why? Because He understood the power of His words. In fact, look at what Jesus said when the disciples commented on it:

> And Peter, remembering, said to Him, "Rabbi, look! The fig tree which You cursed has withered away." So Jesus answered and said to them, "Have faith in God. For assuredly, I say to you, whoever says to this mountain, 'Be removed and be cast into the sea,' and does not doubt in his heart, but believes that those things he says will come to pass, he will have whatever he says. Therefore I say to you, whatever things you ask when you pray, believe that you receive them, and you will have them" (Mark 11:21-24).

This is one of the most amazing declarations about the power of words in all the Bible. And it came straight from the mouth of Jesus in response to a question about a curse He spoke upon a fig tree!

How did cursing, in the biblical sense of the word, come to mean plain old cussing? Let me give you an example. The relatively mild four-letter-word "damn" is an old King James word. It is also the root of the word "damnation"—the term that describes the horrific state of someone being assigned to eternal punishment and never-ending separation from God. In other words, to be damned is the worst thing that could ever happen to a human being. And yet, people damn others all the time.

Why would anyone speak such a curse upon another? Why would people damn their marriage? Their children? Or even their job or checkbook? And yet it happens every day. We have enough problems. Why would we speak a curse upon any person or thing?

Please stop speaking curses. It is an abomination to God. And it's hurting you. Psalm 109 offers a sobering warning in this regard:

> As he loved cursing, so let it come to him; as he did not delight in blessing, so let it be far from him. As he clothed himself with cursing as with his garment, so let it enter his body like water, and like oil into his bones (vv. 17-18).

God's Word is declaring that those who prefer speaking curses to speaking blessing will have lots of the former and very little of the latter.

Do you understand that every time you spew curses out it is like a fountain, and more gets on you than on whomever you are cursing? Why? Because the curse is coming from inside of you and out of your mouth. You cannot handle mud and remain clean. Likewise, you cannot spew curses without having them touch your mouth.

A recent experience I had illustrates this truth. I took some equipment to someone to have it repaired. This man works out of his house, and I found myself standing in his office listening to a stream of swearing and cursing such as I'd never heard in my life. (That's saying something. I used to travel in a pretty rough crowd.)

This man, just in the course of casual conversation, cursed more times in 10 minutes than I'd heard in the previous 10 years. The torrent of profanity spewing from his mouth was astonishing. Of course, I eventually mentioned my line of work. After that he struggled, with only limited success, to get his swearing under control.

Here's the sad irony of the situation. I had come to the man to get something fixed and here he was cursing it! He cursed the item. He cursed the parts that would be required to repair it. And he cursed the company that would provide those parts.

Because I understand the power of words, once I got back in my car, I prayed and broke the power of every curse he had spoken over my project.

A few days later, I mentioned my experience to someone, and he said, "Oh, I know that guy. He works out of his home because he lost his business. He used to have a shop, but he had to close it down. He's had a really tough time of it."

I don't doubt it. I'm sure his unbridled swearing turned off many customers. Nor do I doubt for a moment that, at a deeper level, his constant cursing of his business and everything around him had a powerful spiritual effect.

The sad thing is that he is very good at what he does, but his mouth has brought ruin to his life.

As the psalmist said, "He loved cursing, so let it come to him."

Symptom #7 – Using God's Name in a Self-Serving Way

Like lying, taking the Lord's name in vain is an offense so serious that God made it one of the Ten Commandments:

> You shall not take the name of the LORD your God in vain, for the LORD will not hold him guiltless who takes His name in vain (Exod. 20:7).

There are essentially two ways you can take God's name in vain. I suspect you know about the first one. But you may not even be aware of the second and most common way people commit this sin.

The first way involves using God's name as a curse word. To do so is not only a sign of uncouth manners and a profane mind—it's also a serious offense before God. But before you congratulate yourself on not being a practitioner of this sin, you need to take a closer look at what it means to take the Lord's name in vain.

One of the primary meanings of the word "vain" is "to do something in a self-serving way." Thus, to use God's name in a self-serving way is to take it "in vain." This is why this sin is so similar to blasphemy, which means to use God's name in an unsacred or dishonest way.

For example, when you tell someone "God told me . . ." for self-serving reasons, you're on thin ice. I hear people doing this all the time. They want to convince someone to do something or think something, so they invoke God's name to give their case more weight. It's very tempting to justify your decisions and your choices by saying, "God told me." Here's what God actually does say: Woe to the ones who say, "thus says the Lord," when the Lord has not spoken (see Ezek. 13:7;22:28). Why do such people qualify for a "woe"? Because they are using God's name in a vain way.

Many a desperate single guy has sent a woman in his church's singles' group running for the hills by saying, "God told me that you're the one I'm going to marry." (Note to single guys: If God really had told you that, keep it to yourself. That way you won't mess up the deal before God can speak to her.)

"God told me," may be the most abused phrase in church circles. Certainly avoid using God's name as a curse word, but be just as diligent to avoid using His name in a self-serving way.

Symptom #8 – Spewing Sewer Speech

In the 1939 film *Gone with the Wind*, Clark Gable's line "Frankly, Scarlett, . . ." was considered shocking. Today, television sets and mp3 players routinely spew language so vile that it staggers the imagination. In just a couple of generations, our culture has thrown off all restraint and eliminated all boundaries where obscenity is concerned.

Do you understand how filthy our generation has become in our speech? This represents the eighth sin in our list—it is what the Bible calls "filthy language" (see Eph. 5:3-4).

It is also mentioned in Colossians 3:8: "But now you must also put off all these: anger, wrath, malice, blasphemy, filthy language out of your mouth."

Paul was warning Christian people in his day against this problem. It's a warning we need today as well. When you live in a culture that bombards you with filthy speech, night and day, it's easy to participate in it.

Humor was invented by God. But in case you haven't noticed, in the last 30 years, humor has gotten more and more filthy. People don't believe they can be funny without being perverse. That means you may have opportunities in the workplace or in the marketplace to hear off-color jokes. Listen to me. It's wrong for you to say these things, and it's wrong for you to listen to it.

You may say, "If I don't at least listen to it in my office, they'll call me a goody-goody." I don't care what they call you. I do care what God calls you. And God calls people who use filthy language abominable, detestable and idolatrous. Don't do it.

Symptom #9 – Habitually Speaking Strife

The ninth item on our list is "contentious speech." My thesaurus associates the following words with the word "contentious": "belligerent," "argumentative," "combative," "quarrelsome," "bellicose" and "cantankerous." How's that for a list! Not surprisingly, the Bible records some warnings about allowing such words to characterize our communication.

> It is better to dwell in a corner of a housetop, than in a house shared with a contentious woman (Prov. 21:9).

But don't think that the Bible singles out only women where this sin is concerned:

> As charcoal is to burning coals, and wood to fire, so is a contentious man to kindle strife (Prov. 26:21).

Like most of the other sins on this list of deadly sins, contentious speech is a habit. Some people have simply fallen into the habit of arguing. For them it has become instinctive. And they enjoy it.

Would you like to find out if you have this evil habit? Just ask your spouse (and encourage an honest answer). No one knows better than your spouse if you've cultivated an argumentative spirit.

Do you always have to be right? Do you always have to say the last word? Do you always have to say, "I told you so"? These are all symptoms of a contentious spirit, which will certainly manifest itself as contentious speech.

A friend of mine jokingly says of himself, "I can be wrong, but I'm never in doubt." At least he's self-aware. A lot of people are like that and don't know it. And no one wants to be around a person who argues all the time.

Purpose to develop an agreeable spirit. I'm not suggesting that you have to agree with everything everyone says. I'm simply saying that you're not obligated to correct them! No one has appointed you Earth's guardian of truth and accuracy.

One week when I was preparing to preach on this very subject, I was chatting with two of my children, and one of them asked what I was going to preach about on the weekend. I said, "I'll be talking about why we shouldn't have a contentious spirit, which means being prone to argue and contradict others." Then I helpfully added, "You know, the two of you have a problem in that area from time to time." Their response? In unison they said, "No, we don't."

Symptom #10 – Spreading Pessimism

The last deadly sin on our list may be the most common of all sins of the tongue. It is *unbelief.* Of course, the source of all unbelief is the heart. But as we've seen, if it is in your heart, it will invariably come out of your mouth. And as this passage in Hebrews shows us, the cure for unbelief is also in our mouths:

> Beware, brethren, lest there be in any of you an evil heart of unbelief in departing from the living God; but *exhort* one another daily, while it is called "Today," lest any of you be hardened through the deceitfulness of sin (3:12-13, emphasis added).

There are two things in the passage: first, a warning against having an "evil heart of unbelief," and second, the antidote "exhort one another daily."

How do you exhort others? With your mouth, of course. You use your words to encourage others.

Unbelief is contagious, and it is spread through negativity. If you have a negative mouth, you have a heart of unbelief.

I've actually heard people defend and justify their negativity in the following way, actually presenting it as a virtue! They say, "Well, you know, I'm surrounded by all these positive people, so they need me to be a balancing factor." Or, "My wife is such an optimist and idealist, someone has to be the realist in our home."

This thinking is simply rationalization and self-justification for having a negative, unbelieving heart. Why does any believer have to be negative when God is on the throne and all His promises are "yes" and "amen" (see 2 Cor. 1:20)?

My friend Pastor Jimmy Evans says, "Negativity is simply the devil's language spoken by those who have his perspective." God's language is faith. Nothing is impossible with God (see Matt. 19:26). God never speaks negatively. He speaks truth. Even when He speaks truth, He speaks it by faith, because He sees what can happen.

Faith doesn't mean that you don't see the problem. Faith means you can see past the problem to the answer. You're not saying, "There is no problem." You're saying, "There is an answer!"

By the way, this is where some in the faith movement went too far. We were told that we shouldn't ever say, "I'm sick." I understand the heart of this teaching. But the fact is, you can avoid saying "I'm sick" all day long and it won't do anything to help you get better. Faith says, "I may be sick, but God is healing me!"

Faith is expressed when you declare, "Yes, I have a problem, but God is helping me overcome it. I'm trusting God. I'm believing His promises."

From beginning to end, the Christian life is about faith. We begin it by faith (see Eph. 2:8-9) and we live it by faith:

I have been crucified with Christ; and it is no longer I who live, but Christ lives in me; *and the life which I now live in the flesh I live by faith in the Son of God,* who loved me and gave Himself up for me (Gal. 2:20-21, *NASB*, emphasis added).

Words of unbelief are dangerous. They go against the very essence of what it means to live as a child of God.

. . . .

There you have them—The Ten Deadly Sins of the Tongue. Thinking through this list with me may have been uncomfortable for you, or even painful. But doing this kind of deep inventory of your words is precisely what you need to do if you are going to experience all of the victory, joy and blessing God wants you to enjoy.

Let us determine to submit our mouths to God. And in those areas of speech in which we have bad habits, let's become accountable and correctable with a trusted confidant.

Now read on! The good news is right around the corner!

Notes

1. A. B. Simpson, *Days of Heaven on Earth: A Daily Devotional to Comfort and Inspire* (Camp Hill, PA: Christian Publications, 1984), n.p.
2. Morgan Blake, quoted in George W. Sweeting, *Who Said That?: More than 2,500 Usable Quotes and Illustrations* (Chicago: Moody Press, 1994), n.p.
3. Ibid.

CHAPTER FIVE

The Troublesome Tongue

The difference between the right word and the almost right word is the difference between lightning and a lightning bug.

MARK TWAIN

Did you know that a chameleon's tongue is twice the length of its body? Or that the tongue of a blue whale weighs more than the average elephant? How about the fact that the human tongue is the strongest muscle in the human body?

Of course, as we've seen up to this point, the power of the human tongue goes far beyond mere physical strength. Its real force lies in its ability to produce words. Throughout this study, we've seen that words matter a great deal. And no writer in the Bible makes this case more forcefully than James.

The book of James is remarkable for several reasons. For one thing, most scholars agree that this particular James was the half-brother of Jesus, which means that he writes from a unique vantage point. By having Jesus as his elder brother, James not only was able to observe Jesus live and implement the principles of pleasing our heavenly Father, but he also saw those principles work!

Church history tells us that James was the first pastor of the fledgling church in Jerusalem, which means that he would have had a pastor's heart. I'm sure that James had a desire to see the people in his church experience victory in their lives. And he knew what it would take for them to overcome the very difficult circumstances that they were about to face. We obviously should pay keen attention to any advice that James has to offer us.

Read through James in one sitting and you'll be struck by how much he emphasizes the power of the tongue and the need to use words wisely. The first three chapters alone of James contain the longest discourse on the tongue in the Bible. In fact, one Bible commentator has pointed out that James mentions 14 different kinds of "tongues," including deceitful tongues, perverse tongues, backbiting tongues, and healthy tongues.[1]

Why is this particular subject so important to James? I believe it is because he had seen, by witnessing the life and ministry of Jesus, just how powerful words can be. All this led James to come up with a list of amazing facts about the tongue. But his are much more serious than the ones I cited at the opening of this chapter. So let's explore some of James's amazing facts about the tongue—and why it can be so troublesome at times.

The Tongue Is Disproportionately Powerful

The third chapter of James begins with a startling warning and remarkable declaration:

> My brethren, let not many of you become teachers, knowing that we shall receive a stricter judgment. For we all stumble in many things. If anyone does not stumble in word, he is a perfect man, able also to bridle the whole body (vv. 1-2)

This should certainly give pause to anyone who aspires to be a Bible teacher or preacher—for James warns that he or she will be held to a higher standard. He even goes on to tie the "stricter judgment" that the teacher or preacher will receive to the enormous power of words: "For we *all* stumble in *many* things" (emphasis added; I think most people would say *amen* to that statement). But then James says something amazing: "If anyone does not stumble in word, he or she is perfect, able also to bridle his or her whole body."

By controlling our tongues, we can control our bodies. What an amazing concept! If you are looking for the perfect diet—look no further! If you have a problem with addiction—here's your answer! If you are struggling with lust—you can be free! All you need to do is control your tongue.

This leads us to the first of James's amazing facts about the tongue: *It is disproportionately powerful.* The operative word in this statement is "disproportionately." In other words, what James is saying is that while the tongue is extremely small in proportion to the rest of the body, it has greater influence than any other part of the body. This is a point that James obviously wants us to get, because he then goes on to give us three vivid analogies illustrating the tongue's disproportionate power: (1) It is like a bridle that controls a horse; (2) it is like a rudder that steers a ship; and (3) it is like a spark that has the power to burst into flame and consume an entire forest.

The Tongue Is a Bridle

James's first analogy compares the tongue to a bit or a bridle in a horse's mouth:

> Indeed we put bits in horses' mouths that they may obey us, and we turn [or control] their whole body (Jas. 3:3).

This analogy is one that I can really appreciate. I grew up owning horses, so I understand how, with a little piece of metal called a bit, you can control the superior strength of a large horse and direct the creature where you will.

In essence, this Scripture is saying that our tongue controls our strength and direction. If we're going in the wrong direction, it is because our tongue is leading us there. If we don't have strength to meet the demands of life, it is directly related to the words that we are speaking.

Let's take James's analogy one step further. Think about how a wild horse behaves. The horse is virtually aimless, never going anywhere in particular. It never arrives at a specific destination, because it has none. A wild horse doesn't provide any useful service such as carrying a person or load to a location. Seen in this light, a wild horse has no purpose, no direction, and no lasting value.

James implies that the same is true of us if we fail to bridle our tongue! It's obvious, isn't it? If we don't bridle our tongues, we'll never accomplish the purposes of God in our lives. We'll never experience true and lasting success. In James 1:26, this same concept is stated in even stronger terms: "If anyone among you thinks he's religious [meaning an effective, pleasing server of God] and does not bridle his tongue, but deceives his own heart, this one's religion is useless."

Wow! That's stout stuff! Is it possible that there are Christians who are spending lots of time and energy working for God but, because they don't have any control over their tongues, are really useless in God's kingdom? I'm afraid that is precisely what James is saying. We need to ask ourselves this: *Are we wandering aimlessly like an unbridled horse? Do we think we are serving God but are deceived in our hearts? Is our service useless?*

James boldly challenges each of us to evaluate our lives, and he uses the analogy of a bit in a horse's mouth to make his point unmistakable. Our tongues truly are disproportionately powerful. They can help us achieve God's plan and purpose for our lives, or they can keep us running aimlessly about, accomplishing little to nothing.

The Tongue Is a Rudder

In case the horse metaphor doesn't connect with some of his readers, James uses another word picture to communicate this idea: a ship and its rudder. James 3:4-5 states:

Look also at ships: although they are so large and are driven by fierce winds, they are turned by a very small rudder wherever the pilot desires. Even so the tongue is a little member and boasts great things.

If you've ever been on a cruise (or just seen a large ship), you can easily understand how disproportionately small a rudder is in comparison to the ship. When my family and I went on our first ocean cruise a number of years ago, I was astounded at the size of the ship! It was like a floating city. There were stores, restaurants, a movie theater, and even a bowling alley. It was an enormous vessel. We were impressed at the time, but now (with technology being what it is) some ships also boast inline-skating tracks, climbing walls, Internet lounges, video arcades and ice-skating rinks.

The Titanic was larger than many modern cruise ships. At the time it was built, it was the largest moving object ever constructed by man. It was 882 feet long and stood 11 stories high. It's hard to wrap our minds around the size of that kind of sailing ship. But what may be harder still to reconcile is the fact that a rudder only 78 feet long steered the enormous vessel.

When we consider this, it is easy to recognize how powerful a small rudder can be. Yet James says that the tongue is that disproportionately powerful too!

As a bridle or bit in a horse's mouth controls the horse's direction, so the rudder controls the direction of a ship. How important do you think the rudder of a ship is during foul weather? If you know anything about sailing, you know that it is vital. A ship must be turned into the direction of the wind and waves during a storm or it will capsize and sink.

In the same way, when storms occur in your life, what you say matters! You must meet a crisis head on by speaking the Word of God, not verbally fretting about the worst-case scenario. Maybe one reason why you may have capsized during one of your life's storms is because of your mouth. Maybe you found yourself in a storm and your mouth didn't point you in the right direction. One big wave came along and you were capsized.

As we did with the horse's bridle, let's take James's ship metaphor a bit further. You need a rudder not only when you are sailing in a storm but also in fair weather. Imagine that you and your family have packed a picnic lunch and are heading for the lake on a beautiful sunny Saturday morning. Everyone is excited to be going out in the brand-new sailboat. There is a slight breeze, the water is fairly calm, and it's nice and warm— the perfect day for sailing. Your family steps onboard and gets situated. All life preservers are on, and you shove off.

The kids squeal with delight as the breeze billows out the sails. You glide along at a steady pace for a while, enjoying the experience. Up ahead and to the right, you notice a nice sandy beach that would make a great picnic spot. That's where you want to go. You want to steer in that direction . . . but there isn't a rudder to take you there.

Not only do you sail past the perfect spot, but you also soon realize that there is no way to turn the boat around to head back home. There is no way you can reach your destination without a rudder! You are at the mercy of the wind.

In Ephesians 4:14, Paul tells us that immature believers are people who are blown about by every wind of doctrine. In a similar way, people who can't control their tongues can't control their lives.

It may be difficult to imagine that something as small as your tongue actually has the power to determine the direction of your life. But it does. If you are going in the right direction, it's because your tongue is going in the right direction. If you're going in the wrong direction, it's because your rudder—your tongue—is turned in the wrong direction. In other words, what you've said in the past has framed the life you are experiencing today. You are living your words. *What you say today will steer you toward your tomorrow.* There is destiny in your words!

The Tongue Is a Spark

As a final analogy to show the disproportionate power of the tongue, James compares the tongue to a small spark:

> Even so the tongue is a little member and boasts great things. See how great a forest a little fire kindles! And the tongue is a fire, a world of iniquity. The tongue is so set among our mem-

bers that it defiles the whole body, and sets on fire the course of nature; and it is set on fire by hell (Jas. 3:5-6).

This analogy is very appropriate when you consider that something as small and seemingly insignificant as a spark has the ability to destroy an entire forest. This truth really hit home when my family was vacationing in Yellowstone National Park a few years ago. During our visit, we saw animals that you only see on the Discovery Channel—bears and herds of buffalo, elk, deer and moose. It wasn't hard to imagine fur trappers of old stomping around those cold mountain streams in search of coveted beaver pelts. Grand old fir, spruce and pine trees towered above the forests, and the Rocky Mountains loomed majestically in the background. The wild and untamed views were breathtaking.

As we were driving through the park, drinking in this beautiful scenery and "oohhing" and "ahhing" along the way, we were suddenly met with a heartbreaking sight as we topped a hill. There before us were thousands of acres of charred land. There was nothing but charcoal-black stumps as far as the eye could see.

With absolutely no wildlife visible, this desolate area was a jarring contrast to the land teeming with life that we had just been enjoying. And to think that this destruction probably began with a tiny little spark, possibly from a cigarette being carelessly flicked out the window of a car. According to one report, it takes approximately 11 years for a forest to begin to grow back after such a devastating fire. And many decades will pass before it is truly restored.

Our uncontrolled tongues have the power to create similar devastation in our lives and in the lives of others. That's sobering, isn't it? Often, we open our mouths without thinking about the consequences. We think that what we said was just a little thing—only a little spark carelessly flicked about. But here's the truth: That little spark has the power to cause massive ruin that can be felt for years down the road.

The bit. The rudder. The spark. Each analogy gives us insight into the first of James's amazing facts about the tongue—that it is disproportionately powerful. But of course, there's more!

The Tongue Is Bad from Birth

James continues with the incendiary theme from the previous verse to bring us the second amazing fact about the tongue:

> And the tongue is a fire, a world of iniquity. The tongue is so set among our members that it defiles the whole body, and sets on fire the course of nature; and it is set on fire by hell (Jas. 3:6).

James tells us that the *tongue is inherently evil*. In other words, our tongues are a problem from the day we are born. Think about it: No one has to teach a toddler to lie, say mean things to his sister, or be disrespectful. It all comes so naturally. As soon as we're able to form words, our tongues are there to help get us into trouble. To use the language of computer software, the default setting of the human tongue is "evil."

Think back to your junior high school years. What were your most distinct memories? If you're like most people, your memories probably include hurtful or embarrassing words that were spoken to you by others. For some reason, the wickedness of the human tongue seems to find its fullest expression during the junior high years. I suspect that the reason for this is because as we get older, good manners and social constraints cause us to rein in our tongues a little bit. But when we're 13, we just let the words fly.

You probably remember having all of your physical differences cruelly pointed out to you when you were an adolescent. Maybe you wore glasses or braces or you were taller, shorter, skinnier or heavier than most people—and each of these things were pointed out to you in creative and less-than-flattering ways.

For example, when I was a teenager—and this may be hard for people who know me now to believe—I was the super-skinny kid in the class.

"Hey, Robert!" kids would say to me, "If you turn sideways and stick your tongue out, you'll look like a zipper."

"Hey, Robert! I bet you have to run around in the shower to get wet."

"Hey, Robert! Here's a Cheerio. Use it for a hula hoop!"

I was never given a chance to forget how different I looked. You probably have vivid memories of that kind of "encouragement" as well. I think Winston Churchill had this kind of humor in mind when he said, "A joke is a very serious thing." Indeed, a joke is deadly serious when the joke's on us.

The Tongue Is Humanly Untamable

This brings us to James's third amazing fact: *The tongue is humanely untamable.* We find this fact stated in the next two verses:

> For every kind of beast and bird, of reptile and creature of the sea, is tamed and has been tamed by mankind. But no man can tame the tongue. It is an unruly evil, full of deadly poison (Jas. 3:7-8).

Have you ever sworn to yourself to never, ever say something stupid again? I've taken that oath on many occasions, usually immediately after really sticking my foot in my mouth. If, like me, you've made such an oath to never say dumb things again, you know that it is an impossible vow to keep. Sure, by employing every ounce of willpower you possess, you may be able to stop staying dumb things for about two weeks. But I have learned this scientific truth the hard way: Dumb stores up!

Let me explain. Based on my *extensive scientific research*, I've learned that each of us has what I call a "dumb locker" on the inside. When that locker gets full, it bursts. When that happens, in a single day a person can make up for all the bad words he didn't say in the last three weeks!

James says that no man can tame the tongue. Six thousand years of recorded human history bears out the truth of this statement. And, as James tells us, the tongue isn't just an evil—it's an unruly evil! It's bad enough to have something evil walking around your house and your workplace, but an *unruly* evil? Well, that's a real problem. (By the way, if something is no longer unruly, is it now *ruly*? Just wondering.)

The tongue is *humanly* untamable. That's the bad news. But all is not lost. The good news is that the tongue is *divinely* tamable—the One who made it can tame it! (In the next chapter, we'll look at some of the ways God helps us tame our tongues—and what our role is in that process.)

The Tongue Is
Contrastingly Productive

Let's continue on to the fourth amazing fact about the tongue, which
James discusses in the next few verses:

> With it [our tongue] we bless our God and Father, and with it we
> curse men, who have been made in the similitude of God. Out of
> the same mouth proceed blessing and cursing. My brethren,
> these things ought not to be so. Does a spring send forth fresh
> water and bitter from the same opening? Can a fig tree, my
> brethren, bear olives, or a grapevine bear figs? Thus no spring
> yields both salt water and fresh (Jas. 3:9-12).

I can almost see James shaking his head in sad disbelief as he writes
the words: "Out of the same mouth proceed blessing and cursing."
James is bringing us the fourth amazing fact: *The tongue is contrastingly
productive.*

Once again, the adverb is what's important here—"contrastingly."
The point is not just that the tongue is productive—it certainly is that,
for it can produce fruit and things that will last for a long time—but that
it is *contrastingly* productive. The tongue is unnatural. It can do something that nature cannot.

No tree can produce two kinds of fruit. A fig tree only bears figs.
A grapevine only bears grapes. If a grapevine would bear a fig—or a fig tree
bear grapes—that would be freakish. Unnatural. Likewise, a spring cannot have both salt water and fresh water coming out of the same opening. Yet this is exactly what the tongue can do. From our fallen natures,
the human tongue can spring forth both blessing and cursing—sometimes in the same breath! And, as James points out, that cursing is usually directed at people—people loved by, and made in the image of, God.
People Jesus treasured so much that He laid down His life for them.

This is unnatural, James says. But unnatural for whom? Unnatural
for children of God! This is what the Holy Spirit, writing through James,

is saying: "Brothers and sisters, you're believers now. Stop this! Don't allow the same mouth that blesses and praises God one minute be used to curse and belittle a precious fellow saint the next. That's unnatural. It simply should not be so."

Speaking Life

James has given us four amazing facts about the tongue to consider: The tongue is (1) disproportionately powerful, (2) inherently evil, (3) humanly untamable, and (4) contrastingly productive. Put together, these four truths lead us to a central truth about our words:

> Death and life are in the power of the tongue, and those who love it will eat its fruit (Prov. 18:21).

Wow! I think that's one of the most amazing verses in the Bible. "Death and life are in the power of the tongue." Our words not only impact our own life (for good or for ill), but our tongue also carries the very power of life and death itself! Because we were created in the image of a God who spoke with creative power, our words have power. This is why it's so important that we understand what James is trying to tell us about our tongues. This is why it's so important for us to learn to control our tongues.

For five full chapters now, I've been stepping on your toes and delivering the hard, bad news about how much death and destruction our out-of-control tongues are wreaking on ourselves and others. You're due for some good news, so let me offer you some: Although death is in the power of the tongue, so is life!

Life is in the power of the tongue—*your tongue!* The life that you need in your marriage is in your tongue. The life that you need in your finances is in your tongue. The life that your body needs is in your tongue. And— please get this—the life that your children need is in your tongue.

If you have a child who's away from God, the life that child needs is in your tongue. Why would you ever say, "I have a child who's so stubborn and hard-headed that he'll probably never surrender to God."

Don't speak curses over your children. Instead, say this: "I've got a strong-willed child, and if you read the Bible, those are the ones who make the best disciples. Once that will gets surrendered to God, no amount of peer pressure will be able to move him!"

In this chapter, we've seen how the power of hell wants to control your tongue. Listen to me. Satan wants to occupy your mouth. Why? Because he wants to burn up your God-given destiny and the destinies of everyone around you. That's why the basic theme of this book is: Stop speaking death. Start speaking life!

What does it mean to "speak life?" When I was preparing the material that resulted in this book, I asked the Lord for an example to illustrate this point. I prayed, "Lord, point me toward an example of someone who spoke life over a very hopeless situation and saw it change radically." I thought He might direct me to one of the great figures of the Bible, or perhaps to one of the famous people from Church history. But when the Holy Spirit actually brought the person to my mind, I began to weep.

The greatest example of this I have ever seen is my wife, Debbie.

Years ago, when I was still a selfish and arrogant know-it-all, she began to say things like:

"Robert is a great husband."
"Robert is a good man."
"Robert is an excellent father."
"Robert is a great provider."
"Robert loves people and wants to help them."
"Robert is a great man of God."

She would say things like that all the time. And please understand, when she started saying these things, few of them were even remotely true. In fact, there was abundant evidence to the contrary.

Debbie wasn't lying. She wasn't in denial. She was just unfailingly speaking life to me and over me. And today, those things are much, much closer to being true. I haven't arrived quite yet. I'm still a work in progress. But oh, how far I've come.

That's why I began to cry when the Holy Spirit pointed to this shining example right under my nose. I have had someone who loves me and has spoken life over me for more than 25 years now. And I am a changed man. That's the power of words of life.

That power is in your tongue.

Note
1. Finis Jennings Dake, Sr., *The Dake Annotated Reference Bible* (Lawrenceville, GA: Dake Publishing; June, 1989).

Taming the Tongue

You know you haven't stopped talking since I came here?
You must have been vaccinated with a phonograph needle!
GROUCHO MARX, *DUCK SOUP*

Does the name Antoine Yates ring a bell? Probably not, but a few years ago, he experienced his 15 minutes in the limelight. According to news reports, Mr. Yates had to be hospitalized because he had been attacked by his pet—a cat named "Ming."

Ming was a 400-pound Bengal-Siberian mix tiger that Yates had raised from a cub . . . in his New York City apartment. That's right. The man was living in a cramped New York apartment with a full-grown tiger. At this point, you may be wondering about the soundness of Mr. Yates's judgment.

Well, there is one other detail of this story I haven't mentioned. When police showed up at Mr. Yates's apartment to sedate and take away the tiger, they first had to contend with Mr. Yates's *other* pet—a five-foot long alligator. I'd say Mr. Yates needs someone else to pick out his pets for him.

Some animals are easy to domesticate. Others can be trained and controlled with some difficulty. But some can't be tamed at all. You'll probably never see a trained scorpion on a leash. And I doubt you'll ever find yourself at Seaworld watching a smiling young biologist in a wetsuit riding on the back of a Great White shark.

But among every living, active thing on Earth, there may be nothing as wild, unpredictable and dangerous as the human tongue. It's simply not within our power to tame it. As we saw in the previous chapter, the book of James confirms this:

> For every kind of beast and bird, of reptile and creature of the sea, is tamed and has been tamed by mankind. But no man can tame the tongue. It is an unruly evil, full of deadly poison (3:7-8).

So what's the point, Robert? you may be thinking. *If it's impossible to tame my tongue, why am I even reading this book?* Don't despair! Notice that I said it's not within *our* power to tame it. Taming the tongue is not humanly possible, but the good news is that God is not human. He *can* tame the tongue. After all, God created the tongue, and He wrote the owner's manual. He knows how to get the job done. He said so explicitly in Exodus 4:10-12, where we read this remarkable exchange between God and Moses:

> Then Moses said to the Lord, "O my Lord, I am not eloquent, neither before nor since You have spoken to Your servant; but I am slow of speech and slow of tongue." So the Lord said to him, "Who has made man's mouth? Or who makes the mute, the deaf, the seeing, or the blind? Have not I, the Lord? Now therefore, go, and I will be with your mouth and teach you what you shall say."

Although I have read the book of Exodus many times, there is a remarkable phrase in this passage that I had never noticed until recently. Moses said to God, "I'm not eloquent," by which Moses meant "I don't have a tame tongue." But notice that Moses then goes on to say that this was the case both *before* and *after* God spoke to him on the mountainside.

This is something to which I can certainly relate. I had a problem with my tongue before I came to Christ, and I continued to have a problem with my tongue after I met Him! That's why it's such a thrill to read God's response. The Lord basically says to Moses, "Who made your mouth, son? I'm the one who can make the blind see and even the mute speak. So go! I'll be with your mouth. I'll teach you what to say."

What an amazing promise directly from the lips of God: "I will be with your mouth." I love the fact that God can be with our mouths every moment of every day and teach us what to say. We cannot tame our tongues, but we can submit our words to the Lord and allow Him to tame them.

In the book of Mark, we find a Scripture that confirms how the Holy Spirit can fill our mouths with the right words. Jesus was speaking to His disciples before sending them out to witness. He said:

> But when they arrest you and deliver you up, do not worry
> beforehand, or premeditate what you will speak. But whatever is
> given you in that hour, speak that; for it is not you who speak,
> but the Holy Spirit (Mark 13:11).

Here we see that the Holy Spirit can give us the right words to say. Perhaps you've experienced that very thing when talking to a person who had a great need in his or her life. Suddenly, you were able to speak just the right words to that person; you knew it in your spirit and you knew it because of the person's reaction. And you thanked God, because you had never thought of those words before.

No, you can't tame your tongue, but God can when you submit it to Him. And the agent God will use to do that is His Holy Spirit. In a later chapter, I'll go into some detail about how to fully release the Holy Spirit's power in your life. But for the time being, just know that when God, the Holy Spirit, begins to operate in power in your life—as He did in the lives of the men and women of the New Testament—the first place He will begin to work is in the realm of your words.

I submit my tongue to God, the Holy Spirit, every day. And every day He helps me tame the untamable.

Bridling the Tongue

As a pastor, I love hearing from the smallest members of my congregation. And often the things they say and write are very funny. Art Linkletter was right—kids do say the darnedest things! For example, a while back I received a letter from a child in my church inviting me to a Pastors' Appreciation Night at his school. It read:

> *Dear Pastor Robert,*
>
> *Please come to our Pastor Appreciation Night. We'll have spaghetti and blankets.*

Spaghetti and blankets, eh? Well, that's an offer simply too appealing to pass up! Spaghetti yes. Blankets, sure. But spaghetti and blankets together? What time do you want me there?! Oh, and he added a little addendum to the end of his letter:

> *P.S. Please come. It's the last thing in my life I'm living for.*

Ah, a flair for the dramatic too! As a preacher, I have to respect that. Of course, the little guy will get even more proficient with his language as he grows up. And in the same way, when we submit to God and allow Him to transform our life, we will grow in our control over our tongues and the constructive use of our tongues.

That's what I want you to see right now. Just because James tells us that no person, in his own power, can tame the tongue, it doesn't mean that we carry no responsibility for our words. We can't just say, "Well, it's a hopeless cause, so I'm just going to go ahead and say whatever I please. I'll just hope that one day God will step in and tame it for me."

The truth is, we can—and we must—cooperate with God in this process. It's very possible to allow the Holy Spirit to tame our mouths. Of course, it's important to recognize that mastery of our words will be a *process*—it won't be something that we will be able to achieve overnight. Just as when we were young and had to grow and progress in our use of the English language, we will have to grow and progress in the mastery over our tongues.

Recall that one of the metaphors James used was that of a bit in a horse's mouth. I challenge you: Go catch a wild mustang on the plains of West Texas and put a bit between that horse's teeth. Will he instantly become tame? Will his behavior and body language indicate that he's thinking, *Hey, where has this been all my life? This cold metal feels great here in my mouth. Thank you so much!* Not on your life. In fact, that horse will fight it at first. But over time, he will learn to accept the bit and respond to it. First comes the bridle, and then the taming. And it takes time.

What I'm suggesting is that when we begin to bridle our tongue, we won't find it instantly tamed and under control. It's going to take a while. And ultimately, it will be the power and grace of God that will tame our tongue. But for that to happen, we must first learn to *bridle* it. Why? Because God will never override our freedom to choose. Put another way, human power and strength alone can never tame the destructive power of the tongue, but when we choose to cooperate with God, it is possible.

Thus, *we* are responsible for bridling our tongues. And I believe the Lord has shown me three very practical things that we can do to accomplish this vital step. Think of them as the three pieces of an effective bridle for your tongue.

1. Hold On There Just a Minute

The first essential piece of such a bridle is to cultivate the ability to *pause*. I'm referring to the rare ability to wait and say nothing for a moment while we contemplate the effect of the words we're about to speak. It's not easy. I've seen people literally clap their hands over their mouth in an effort to keep the words from flying out. And we don't have the saying "hold your tongue" for no reason.

To *pause* means to simply not say anything until we know precisely what we should say. I have met some people whom I suspect believe the world will stop orbiting if there is any silence in the air at all. They feel they just have to keep talking. But I can assure you that it's okay to have a thoughtful moment of silence in a conversation. It's okay to simply pause.

Think back to the words of Proverbs 18:21: "Life and death are in the power of the tongue." If words truly wield the power of life and death—and they do—shouldn't you and I pause before we let our words fly toward the hearts of the people with whom we live, work and worship? Is it such an odd thing just to take a moment? Because, like it or not, we're either speaking death or speaking life.

James 1:19 tells us, "Therefore, my beloved brethren, let every man be swift to hear, slow to speak, slow to wrath." If you've ever had a problem with anger, here's the key to keeping your temper under control: If you want to be slow to wrath, be slow to speak and quick to hear. Do you realize that most of us have that backward? Most of us are slow to hear and quick to speak.

Former U. S. President Calvin Coolidge was famous for being a man of few but well-chosen words. It is said that one time a reporter stopped him as he was leaving a church service one Sunday and shouted, "Hey, Mr. President. How did you like the service today?"

"Fine," Coolidge replied.

"What did the minister preach about?"

"Sin."

"Well, what did he say about it?" the reporter persisted.

"He was against it."

On another occasion, Silent Cal (as he came to be known) was at a White House dinner party. He was seated next to a rather loud and talkative lady who eventually turned to him and said, "My husband bet me I couldn't get you to say three words tonight!" Coolidge reportedly turned to her after a moment and simply said, "You lose."

Now, President Coolidge may have taken this principle to an extreme. I'm not talking about being rude or uncommunicative. But pausing to consider our words before we speak is definitely a biblical principle. For example, Proverbs has much to say on this subject. (In fact, the three great themes of the book of Proverbs are our morals, our money and our mouths!)

For example, in Proverbs 21:23, we read, "Whoever guards his mouth and tongue keeps his soul from troubles." That would be an excellent verse to memorize. We ought to say this every morning. Notice that it says "whoever guards his mouth." In other words, it's *our* responsibility to do the guarding.

Another gem from Proverbs 10:19 states, "In the multitude of words, sin is not lacking." The phrase "in the multitude of words" means that we talk a lot and then speak death. Sin is not lacking when we do this. But the next phrase in this verse states that "he who restrains his lips is wise." In other words, there is wisdom in employing the pause principle. And once again, we see that the responsibility is ours. It's not all just on God. We are responsible for what we say.

To remove any lingering doubt about whether learning to pause before speaking carries the God Housekeeping seal of approval, let me offer you one more verse: "He who has knowledge spares his words, and a man of understanding is of a calm spirit. Even a fool is counted wise when he holds his peace" (Prov. 17:27-28). What this verse is saying is that if we're smart, we'll all cultivate a little Calvin Coolidge in our speaking habits.

My father used to quote his own version of the last part of this Scripture to me. He used to say, "Son, if you'd just close your mouth from time to time, people might at least *think* you were smart." He wasn't being unkind. He was honestly trying to help me. And he was exactly right! Mark Twain said it this way: "It is better to keep your mouth closed and let people think you are a fool than to open it and remove all doubt."

Let me present my own East Texas paraphrase of the verses we've just examined: Shut up every once in a while and things will go a lot better for you! If you have a problem saying the wrong thing at the wrong time (as I clearly did growing up), there is something I'd like you to try. Try saying *nothing*. Just stop and don't say anything. Just close your mouth.

In other words . . . pause.

Here's one of the pitfalls into which I frequently fall: When someone is talking to me, I begin to think about what I'm going to say in response. But the moment I start focusing on what I want to say, I've stopped truly listening to the other person. This, of course, can lead to some embarrassing moments. Often, the person who is speaking to me will suddenly say something like, "So, how would you handle that,

Robert?" My stammering, hedging, floundering response quickly expos-
es the fact that I wasn't really listening. I think Leo Buscaglia had this
phenomenon in mind when he said, "Most conversations are just alter-
nating monologues. The question is, Is there any real listening going on?"

Pause. It is the first key to bridling the tongue.

2. Let's Give That Some Thought

Once we've paused before speaking, we're ready to take the next step in
successfully bridling our tongue: *ponder*.

There are essentially three types of people in the world: (1) Those
who think *before* they speak; (2) Those who think *while* they speak; and
(3) Those who think *after* they speak. (Having written that, I now realize there may actually be a fourth type: Those who just speak—and *never*
think. I've met a few of those types of people over the years.)

Which one do you have a tendency to be? When people describe
you, do they say, "You know what I like about her? She always thinks
before she talks. She never runs off at the mouth." Is that what people
say about you? Or do you tend to think *while* you talk—evaluating and
weighing your words as they are coming out of your mouth? Or do you
think *after* you talk—often only realizing later that what you said was
hurtful, insensitive or inappropriate?

No matter what type of pattern you have followed in the past, you
can change. You can train yourself to think before you speak.

I have a dear friend—one of the elders at the church that I pastor—
who I frequently call for advice, counsel, or simply to hear his perspective. Over the years, he's proven to be extremely wise and discerning.
As I was writing this chapter, I realized that my friend almost never
responds to my questions immediately. Invariably when I ask him a
question, he will respond, "Okay, Robert, I understand your question.
Let me think about it for a bit and I'll get back to you." He simply does
not give me an off-the-cuff response but insists on taking the opportunity to think before he speaks. Perhaps that's why he is known for his
wisdom—and why I continue to seek out his advice.

We all can be more like my wise friend if we purposefully choose to
be people who reflectively think about what we say before we say it.

If we choose to be people who first pause, and then ponder. Doing these two things will position us to employ the third key to bridling our tongue.

3. Appeal to a Higher Authority

I bet you've already anticipated the next element. After you pause and ponder, but before you speak, it's time to *pray*.

The sixth chapter of Isaiah provides us with some insight as to why this is so important. In this passage of Scripture, Isaiah has just been taken up into the throne room of heaven and has seen what no human being has ever fully seen before—the glory of the angelic heavenly host around the throne of God. Isaiah describes this experience as follows:

> In the year that King Uzziah died, I saw the Lord sitting on a throne, high and lifted up, and the train of His robe filled the temple. Above it stood seraphim; each one had six wings: with two he covered his face, with two he covered his feet, and with two he flew. And one cried to another and said: "Holy, holy, holy is the LORD of hosts; the whole earth is full of His glory!" And the posts of the door were shaken by the voice of him who cried out, and the house was filled with smoke (vv. 1-4).

Quite an experience, huh? But what I want you to notice is Isaiah's reaction in the very next verse to this encounter with the awesome King of the Universe:

> Then I said: "Woe is me, for I am undone! Because I am a man of unclean lips, and I dwell in the midst of a people of unclean lips; for my eyes have seen the King, the LORD of hosts" (v. 5).

What was Isaiah's initial gut reaction on seeing the full radiance of God's holiness? He became suddenly and painfully aware of his words! He got convicted about his mouth. And not just for himself, but for his entire nation! In *THE MESSAGE* version of the Bible, Isaiah's words are rendered like this:

Doom! It's Doomsday! I'm as good as dead!
Every word I've ever spoken is tainted—blasphemous even!
And the people I live with talk the same way, using words that
corrupt and desecrate.
And here I've looked God in the face!

Now, watch what happens in the next two verses:

Then one of the seraphs flew to me with a live coal in his hand,
which he had taken with tongs from the altar. With it he
touched my mouth and said, "See, this has touched your lips;
your guilt is taken away and your sin atoned for" (vv. 6-7, *NIV*).

Keep in mind that Isaiah had this experience 700 years before Jesus
would arrive to atone for the sins of all mankind. Yet here we have a foreshadowing of the salvation that Jesus made available to each of us. Isaiah
has an encounter with God, is convicted of his sin, and is then offered
cleansing through the fire of sacrifice. That fiery coal symbolized the
only one who can take away iniquity—Jesus. He's the only one.

Something else came to my mind when I was reading about this
angelic touch of the fire of God. I realized that I need that touch every
morning. I'm not talking about getting saved again and again; but
rather, I'm talking about coming into the presence of God each and
every morning to have Him touch my lips. Wouldn't it be wonderful to
have a holy God sanctify our lips so that we quit speaking death over the
people in our life and instead speak life over them? We can, you know.
It can happen as we engage the presence of God in prayer.

It happened for me for the very first time on the night of February
16, 1981, in Room 12 of Jake's Motel in Kentucky. I was a 19-year-old kid
who was utterly bound up in insecurity, rejection and pride. An evangelist friend with me who was trying to help me sort things out said,
"Robert, maybe you've never laid your insecurity on the cross." At these
words, the Holy Spirit pierced my heart with conviction. "Maybe I've
never laid anything on the cross at all," I replied. "I don't think I've ever
fully surrendered my life to Christ." My friend had to get ready for a

meeting that night, so he said, "Well, I'll just let you work it out with the Lord." And he left.

Alone with God in that shabby little motel room, I prayed this prayer: "God, I just want You to understand who You're getting in this deal. You're getting an immoral person. You're getting a liar. You're getting a dishonest person. You're getting a selfish person. And You need to know something else. I can't change. I've tried my whole life. I've tried to do the right thing and I can't. But if You want me, You can have me."

Not audibly—but in a voice nonetheless clear and unmistakable in my heart—God said to me in response, "I want you and I can change you." At that moment, it was as if God had reached down and picked me up, as you would pick up a little baby. Then He said, "From now on you're Mine. And I will make you more than you can dream."

God changed my heart that day. It is no exaggeration to say that from that moment forward, things were never the same. And in many sweet subsequent encounters with my heavenly Father, I've had a coal from the fires of His love touch my unclean lips and make them fit to speak of His love to a world that He longs to help and heal. The Bible tells us that God has given us a new heart—that we are to put off the old self and put on the new one.

Pause. Ponder. And then pray. Take some time before you speak and let your converted heart and the new person inside of you tell you what to say.

Chopping Down the Tree of Bitterness

Before we leave this discussion, let me mention one more important step in this process: *forgiveness*. There is only one bridge to restoration and healing—and that bridge is forgiveness. It is the only way to get rid of bad words.

If you have spoken words of death instead of life over people, you need to seek forgiveness. If someone has spoken those words to you, you need to extend forgiveness (even if the offending person hasn't asked for it). This truth is so very important.

Wait a minute, Robert, you may be thinking at this point. *Are you really suggesting that I need to forgive people who haven't even acknowledged that they hurt me?* That is exactly what I am suggesting. If someone has spoken bad words to you, you need to forgive that person even if he or she *never* asks for your forgiveness. If you are unwilling to forgive someone because he or she has never repented or asked you for forgiveness, you're letting a tree grow in you. And that tree is going to produce the fruit of bitterness. The only way to cut down that bad tree is through forgiveness.

All fruit carries seeds, and those seeds hold the potential to create more trees. Lots of them. If the fruit of unforgiveness is in you, that fruit contains seeds that have the potential to produce an entire forest of bitterness over time. I think it's interesting to note that when John the Baptist appeared on the scene and told people to "repent for the kingdom of heaven is at hand" (Matt. 3:2), he also said:

> And even now the ax is laid to the root of the trees. Therefore every tree which does not bear good fruit is cut down and thrown into the fire (v. 10).

Notice that when John talked to people about repentance, he basically said that there are some trees that are going to have to be cut down. Forgiveness is the only tool that can chop down trees of bitterness and offense. Forgiveness is the ax.

The subject of chopped-down trees reminds me of a time early in my ministry when I was desperate for places to preach and teach. I'd take any opportunity, no matter how small the church or how out of the way its location. Sometimes, the directions to these wonderful country churches were a little unusual, but never more so than on one particular occasion.

The pastor of a rural church actually gave me the following directions: "Head East out of town and turn left where the old oak tree used to be. Go North around a mile. You'll cross a bridge. When you cross that bridge, two big dogs will chase your car. When they stop chasing you, turn right, and you'll see the church down on your left."

Of course, first I wondered, *How do I know where the old oak tree used to be? Is there a stump? Are there grieving squirrels? I don't know!* But wouldn't you know it, the rest happened just as he described! The moment we crossed the bridge, two dogs started chasing our car. After a few hundred feet, the dogs got tired and turned back. At that moment, the road to the church appeared on our right.

Allow me to give you some directions that are a little more straight-forward. If you have spoken bad words, you have planted bad trees that are going to bear bad fruit unless you cut them down. And the only way to cut them down is with the ax of repentance and forgiveness.

You must ask for, and give, forgiveness. Your dad may have said something tremendously hurtful to you 50 years ago, but if you haven't forgiven him, you still have a bad fruit-producing tree in your life. And it has been producing that bad fruit for 50 years. Just forgive him. Lay an ax to the root of that tree.

The Persistence of Words

Let me conclude this chapter with some good news about the tongue. Just as bad words are powerful and persistent—good words are even more so. Good words last and carry enormous power to help, heal, encourage and restore. When we learn to pause, ponder and pray before we speak, we learn to speak words of life to others. And when we say words that are positive or encouraging to our spouse, to our kids or to our friends—those words don't evaporate! They last forever.

The apostle Paul knew a little bit about the persistent power of words. In his second letter to Timothy, which basically serves as a letter of encouragement from Paul to his younger friend, Paul writes:

> I thank God, whom I serve with a pure conscience, as my forefa-thers did, as without ceasing I *remember* you in my prayers night and day, greatly desiring to see you, being mindful of your tears, that I may be filled with joy (2 Tim. 1:3-4, emphasis added).

"I *remember* you in my prayers." That may not seem like much to us. The phrase "I'm praying for you" has become little more than a trite cliché in many Christian circles. But I can assure you that when the apostle Paul wrote those words to Timothy, it meant the world.

You see, when Paul wrote this passage, he used a Greek word that we need to understand—the one translated into English as "remember." The root of this Greek word is *mnema*, which is a word that refers to a memorial or a sepulcher. In other words—it refers to a headstone for a grave! Although this sounds a bit dark at first, think about the reason why we put up headstones—so that we can remember a person's life and how he or she was special to us.

Young Timothy was obviously going through a time of trial or trouble. Paul was mindful of his tears. But Paul did much more than just say, "Hey, I'm prayin' for ya there, buddy." He said that he was *holding* Timothy and his situation up before God. He was saying that he had laid hold of Timothy's need and was maintaining it before the throne of heaven. In a very real sense, Paul was saying, "I'm erecting a monument before God where you are concerned—a memorial to your need."

Our prayers, like Paul's, don't just dissipate after we pray them. They persist as a memorial in heaven before God. This is why a grandmother can pray for her grandchild for years, die and go to heaven, and that grandchild will come to Christ 20 years later. Her prayers became a memorial before God. And in due time, God honored them.

Good words last, too. Don't stop praying for your family or your marriage. You are building a memorial—a monument before God. Cultivate the practice of encouraging, praising and honoring with the fruit of your lips.

CHAPTER SEVEN

The Baptism of Heaven

God commands us to be filled with the Spirit; and if we aren't filled,
it's because we're living beneath our privileges.
D. L. MOODY

By now, it is my sincere hope that you are convinced about the importance of your words, because the bottom line is this: Words hold the key to blessing in your life. And yet, as we saw in the last chapter, "no man can tame the tongue." In other words, what we desperately need to do—get our mouths under control—is utterly impossible through human willpower and determination alone.

But let's suppose for a moment that there was something available to you that would not only help you control your words but also give you the power to live a more victorious life. Would you be interested in knowing how to receive it?

No doubt the answer is yes!

There is such a power available to you. God has made a way for you not only to become His child through the experience of salvation but also to receive what I call "the baptism of heaven," which will equip you to live every aspect of the Christian life more fully and powerfully. What is the baptism of heaven? It occurs when you are filled with the Holy Spirit and receive the power of God in your life.

Yes, I know this subject is somewhat controversial in some quarters, but I must share it with you. Why? Because a book that hopes to help you turn your tongue into a fountain of life rather than a fire hose of destruction simply would not be complete without pointing you to the only source of supernatural help available on planet Earth. And I'm not just referring to *help*. I'm talking about "the Helper,"—the wonderful person of the Holy Spirit.

Baptism in the Holy Spirit is an important topic in regard to the power of our words. No man can tame the tongue. But the Holy Spirit can! That's why I'm asking you to read this chapter with an open heart and mind and lay aside any preconceived ideas about baptism in the Holy Spirit. Simply allow the Lord to speak to you through the Scriptures that will be presented and then decide for yourself. (By the way, guess which member of the Trinity has the assignment of leading us into all truth? See John 16:13.)

Making the Break: Finney and Moody

We are not the first generation of believers who have faced this question regarding baptism in the Holy Spirit. Charles Finney, the great nineteenth-century evangelist, had to make this break with his doctrinal past at one point in his life. In his autobiography, Finney describes the night it happened:

> As I turned and was about to take a seat by the fire, I received a mighty baptism of the Holy Ghost. Without any expectation of it, without ever having the thought in my mind that there was any such thing for me, without any recollection that I had ever

heard the thing mentioned by any person in the world, the Holy Ghost descended on me in a manner that seemed to go through me, body and soul. I could feel the impression, like a wave of electricity, going through and through me. Indeed it seemed to come in waves and waves of liquid love; for I could not express it in any other way. It seemed like the very breath of God. I can recollect distinctly that it seemed to fan me, like immense wings.[1]

From that point forward, Finney recommended the experience to all believers—especially those who needed to minister with power to others. Today, Charles Finney is widely considered to be one of the greatest evangelists in Church history.

A few decades later, Dwight L. Moody, another extraordinary evangelist and preacher, also had to decide whether to stay with the religious tradition he had been taught or pursue what he had begun to clearly see in God's Word. He was pastor of a church in which there was no power, little life, and not much happening spiritually. Two little ladies in his congregation who were baptized in the Holy Spirit, Auntie Cook and Mrs. Snow, began praying for him to receive this experience. However, this went against Moody's existing theological belief that people received the Holy Spirit fully when they were saved. So for a season, he more or less dismissed these ladies' entreaties.

Moody couldn't help noticing, however, that there was a certain dimension of power evident in the lives of these ladies that most other Christians didn't possess. So he decided one day to research the Scriptures for himself. As he studied the Bible, he became convinced that there was indeed a separate experience from salvation called the baptism in the Holy Spirit. As his friend and fellow evangelist R. A. Torrey told it later, Moody received his answer without warning one day while strolling down busy Wall Street in New York City.

The power of God fell upon him as he walked up the street and he had to hurry off to the house of a friend and ask that he might have a room by himself, and in that room he stayed alone for hours; and the Holy Ghost came upon him, filling his soul with such joy that at last he had to ask God to withhold His hand, lest he die on the spot from very joy.[2]

From that time forward, Moody found that "the power of God wrought through him mightily in North London, and hundreds were added to the churches."[3] After that experience, Moody always urged his friend Torrey to "preach on the baptism with the Holy Ghost."[4]

Don't you find this interesting? Nothing remarkable happened in Moody's life or ministry until he received the baptism in the Holy Spirit. Afterward, supernatural power was evident in his life! No longer was he working in his own ability and strength. God added His *super* to Moody's *natural* ability.

Baptism into the Body of Christ and Water Baptism

Hebrews 6:1-2 encourages us to leave the discussion of elementary principles and go on to maturity. One of those elementary principles is the doctrine of baptisms. Note that it doesn't say the doctrine of *baptism* (singular), but *baptisms* (plural). So let's begin our quest for the truth by talking about the first of the three baptisms that are mentioned in Scripture: baptism into the Body of Christ. If you are a Christian, you are probably very familiar with this first baptism. The baptism into the Body of Christ occurs when you receive salvation.

First Corinthians 12:13 explains, "For by one spirit we were all baptized into one body." Notice here who the agent of this baptism is. When you received Jesus as your Savior, the Holy Spirit baptized you into the Body of Christ. In other words, when you were saved, *the Holy Spirit baptized you into Jesus.*

The second baptism often discussed in Scripture is water baptism. It's a very powerful and important step in each believer's life—so much so that water baptism is part of the Great Commission that Jesus gave to His followers.

Go therefore and make disciples of all the nations, *baptizing* them in the name of the Father and of the Son and of the Holy Spirit (Matt. 28:19, emphasis added).

Baptism in water follows repentance for your sins, and acknowledgment and acceptance of Jesus as your Savior. Water baptism is a tremendously significant experience in conjunction with salvation. However, if you get water baptized before you actually get saved, you just get wet!

The colorful Sam Houston, one of the founding fathers of my native Texas, knew this experience firsthand. Although he was raised in church, by his own account he really did not get saved until he was an adult and serving as governor of Texas. About two months after he came to Christ, Houston asked his pastor to baptize him in water. The pastor was a little perplexed at this request, because he knew Houston's history. Houston proceeded to explain that when he had been baptized as a young person, he hadn't been born again. He said something to the effect of, "Now I know I'm saved, because I feel a radical change."

So, a service was arranged for the governor. As onlookers lined the banks of a nearby river, the governor and the pastor waded into the water so that Houston could be baptized. The pastor noticed that Houston's wallet was still in his pocket. He asked if Houston wanted to remove it first. To that, the governor replied that he had left it there on purpose. "It needs to be baptized too," he said, and then turned to the crowd and said: "And by the way, a lot of you live as if your wallets need to get baptized."

Baptizing your wallet is a novel idea, but the real point of this story is that water baptism is not just a religious ritual. It is a statement about the change that has occurred in your life as a result of the salvation experience. I like the way the *Amplified Bible* explains this in Colossians 2:12-13:

You were buried with Him in [your] baptism, in which you were also raised with Him [to a new life] through [your] faith in the working of God [as displayed] when He raised Him up from the dead. And you who were dead in trespasses and in the uncircumcision of your flesh (your sensuality, your sinful carnal nature), [God] brought to life together with [Christ], having [freely] forgiven us all our transgressions.

Being saved means that you stop going *your* way and start going *God's* way. Your sinful, carnal nature is buried with Christ (that is what being submerged in water represents), and you are raised up out of the water (as Jesus was raised from the dead) to newness of life. When you get saved, you become a new person in Christ. Being baptized in water demonstrates that your old sin nature is cut off and that all things have become new in your life (see 2 Cor. 5:17).

Still, you must have *power* to live victoriously—which brings us to the third baptism: baptism in the Holy Spirit.

Holy Spirit Baptism

Let me say right up front that I have a lot of empathy for those who contend that baptism into the Body of Christ and water baptism are the only two baptisms the Bible speaks of. I used to contend this as well! I grew up in a church that didn't recognize the Holy Spirit's involvement in people's lives. Later, when I went to Bible college, I was further indoctrinated against it.

Strangely enough, one of the Scriptures that my friends and I quoted to prove that there was no baptism with the Holy Spirit separate from the salvation experience was this passage from Ephesians:

There is one body and one Spirit, just as you were called in one hope of your calling; one Lord, one faith, one baptism; one God and Father of all, who is above all, and through all, and in you all (4:4-6).

As a young Bible school student, I was very smug and sure of myself. I used to point to this verse and say, "See, the Bible says there is only one baptism!" Of course, even as I was saying that, I believed in two baptisms—one into the Body of Christ and one in water.

What I didn't notice back then is that this same verse says "one Lord," even though it is clear that there are three members of the Godhead. In fact, this very same passage of Scripture mentions all three members of the Trinity—one "Spirit," one "Lord," and one "God and Father of all." One God. Three expressions.

In the very same way, there is one baptism but three expressions. There is the baptism into the Body of Christ when we get saved; there is water baptism; and there is baptism in the Holy Spirit. Let's look at more passages from Scripture that support this idea, beginning with the book of Acts. We will also look at examples from the New Testament as well the Old Testament.

Scriptural Support from the Book of Acts

Let's look at an account from the book of Acts that talks about all three baptisms. Here we find that when the people were saved and water baptized, they also got Spirit baptized:

> Now when they heard this, they were cut to the heart, and said to Peter and the rest of the apostles, "Men and brethren, what shall we do?" Then Peter said to them, "Repent [salvation] and let every one of you be baptized in the name of Jesus Christ for the remission of sins [water baptism]; and you shall receive the gift of the Holy Spirit [there's the Spirit baptism.] For the promise is to you and to your children, and to all who are afar off, as many as the Lord our God will call (2:37).

This promise of salvation and the baptism in the Holy Spirit is "to you and to your children, and to all." Yet there are many Christians who do not take advantage of this. There are many people who get saved but are never water baptized, and they also have a doctrinal view that says they don't need to be baptized in the Spirit. What they don't understand is that the baptism in the Holy Spirit adds a supernatural dimension to their lives. Through this baptism, power from on high—the power of the

Holy Spirit of God—comes and dwells within the believer who receives it.
In Acts 8 we find a revival breaking out:

> Then Philip went down to the city of Samaria and preached
> Christ to them. And the multitudes with one accord heeded the
> things spoken by Philip, hearing and seeing the miracles which
> he did. For unclean spirits, crying with a loud voice, came out of
> many who were possessed; and many who were paralyzed and
> lame were healed. And there was great joy in that city (vv. 5-8).

There should always be great joy when people are set free and healed!
There certainly shouldn't be great arguments about it. But sadly, today,
that's often what we have. This revival recorded in Acts 8 sets the stage
for verses 12-13. As you read these verses, watch for the three baptisms
we've been identifying:

> But when they believed Philip as he preached the things con-
> cerning the kingdom of God and the name of Jesus Christ, both
> men and women were baptized. Then Simon himself also
> believed; and when he was baptized he continued with Philip,
> and was amazed, seeing the miracles and signs which were
> done.

Here we obviously have the first two baptisms. People "believed." And then
people "were baptized." Huge segments of the Body of Christ today have
these two baptisms and are convinced they have all they need. In fact, they
have been told that these two baptisms are all there are. They say, "I've
been saved and baptized. I have everything!"

But before you get too settled in that belief, let's read on.

> Now when the apostles who were at Jerusalem heard that
> Samaria had received the word of God, they sent Peter and John
> to them, who, when they had come down, prayed for them that
> they might receive the Holy Spirit. For as yet He had fallen upon
> none of them. They had only been baptized in the name of the

Lord Jesus. Then they laid hands on them, and they received the
Holy Spirit (vv. 14-17).

As we saw in the prior verses, these people had "believed." They had been
baptized. Yet when Peter and John heard about it and came to visit, the
first thing they did was pray "for them to receive the Holy Spirit."
Obviously, Peter and John hadn't gotten the word from denominational headquarters that if you've been saved and baptized, you have everything you need. Once again we see the three baptisms modeled for us in
the Bible.

We see it again in Acts 19.

And it happened, while Apollos was at Corinth, that Paul, having
passed through the upper regions, came to Ephesus. And finding
some disciples he said to them, "Did you receive the Holy Spirit
when you believed?" (v. 1).

The book of Acts covers several decades of Early Church history.
The deeper you get into Acts, the farther away from Jesus' resurrection
you get. The event described above is years after the day of Pentecost.
This is one of those verses that I used to just skip over because it did not
compute. There was no way that I could reconcile this to my doctrinal
position.

Keep in mind that the person asking the question, "Did you receive
the Holy Spirit when you believed?" is the guy who wrote nearly a third
of the New Testament—Paul. You'd think he would know correct doctrine, wouldn't you?

I always laugh when I read this group's response to Paul's question.
Apparently they grew up in the same kind of church I did.

So they said to him, "We have not so much as heard whether
there is a Holy Spirit" (v. 2).

I'm really not trying to make fun of any person or institution, but I'm
always amazed to observe how many Christians grew up in churches

where the Holy Spirit was hardly ever mentioned. In any event, Paul decides to check out their salvation, just to make sure they've received the first two baptisms.

> And he said to them, "Into what then were you baptized?" So they said, "Into John's baptism." Then Paul said, "John indeed baptized with a baptism of repentance, saying to the people that they should believe on Him who would come after him, that is, on Christ Jesus." When they heard this, they were baptized in the name of the Lord Jesus (vv. 3-5).

There we see "repent and believe"—the two components of salvation. And we see water baptism. I bet you can guess what happened next.

> And when Paul had laid hands on them, the Holy Spirit came upon them, and they spoke with tongues and prophesied (v. 6).

There's that vital third element. It's a pattern we see over and over in Scripture. In fact, it would take an entire book on this subject for me to take you through all the places in Scripture where we see this threefold pattern portrayed—literally and symbolically—in the Bible.

New Testament Examples

The Bible is a spiritual book, and those who read it have to read it with spiritual eyes. With that in mind, I want to show you some figurative types of the three baptisms in New Testament Scripture. First, look at 1 John 5:7-8:

> For there are three who bear witness in heaven: the Father, the Word, and the Holy Spirit; and these three are one. And there are three that bear witness on earth: the Spirit, the water, and the blood; and these three agree as one.

According to these verses, there are three heavenly witnesses and three earthly witnesses. To what do they bear witness? To the supernatural—

to the fact that there is a God in heaven who lives, who moves, who loves us! In heaven, the Father, the Word (Jesus), and the Holy Spirit all bear witness to this fact. And as this verse tells us, there are three "on earth who bear witness" as well: "the Spirit, the water, and the blood."

In these three witnesses we see once more the three baptisms. The "blood" refers to salvation, because "without shedding of blood there is no remission" (Heb. 9:22). We're saved by the blood of Jesus.

The "water" clearly points to water baptism. When you are water baptized after salvation, the old person is cut off—in the same way flesh is cut away in circumcision. That's what Romans 6 and Colossians 2 tell us. Baptism is more than a symbol. It's more than a mere act of obedience. Water baptism is a key step in gaining the ability to live in victory over sin.

The third "witness" on Earth is "the Spirit." You'll notice that the Spirit is the only member of the Trinity mentioned as bearing witness both in heaven and on Earth. That's because He is the member who is currently active on the earth today! God is in heaven and Jesus is sitting at His right hand, making intercession for us (see Rom. 8:34).

There is yet another reason we can be sure that baptism into the Body of Christ is different and separate from baptism in the Holy Spirit. It becomes evident when we look closely at two Scriptures, one of which I've already cited.

Recall that 1 Corinthians 12:13 says, "For by one Spirit we were all baptized into one body." Then in Matthew 3:11, John the Baptist, speaking of Jesus, declared that He would baptize us "with the Holy Spirit and fire."

What I want you to notice about these two verses is that in one case, the Spirit baptizes us into Jesus, and in the other, Jesus baptizes us into the Spirit. You don't have to know Greek to see that they can't possibly be talking about the same event. You just need to know English! In the first reference, the Holy Spirit is the subject, or the one doing the baptizing. In the second reference, Jesus is the subject.

So let's review the picture the Bible is painting here. When you are saved, the Holy Spirit baptizes you into Jesus. Then, if you are obedient to the Lord's command, you are baptized in water. Then Jesus baptizes us in the Holy Spirit. Three separate events. You need the first to go to heaven.

You need the second to be obedient. And you need both the second and the third to live a victorious Christian life.

By the way, that third baptism experience is mentioned in *all four Gospels:*

> I indeed baptize you with water unto repentance, but He who is coming after me is mightier than I, whose sandals I'm not worthy to carry. He will baptize you with the Holy Spirit and fire (Matt. 3:11; see also Mark 1:8; Luke 3:16).

> I did not know Him, but He who sent me to baptize with water said to me, "Upon whom you see the Spirit descending, and remaining on Him, this is He who baptizes with the Holy Spirit" (John 1:33).

The wording in John's account is very important, because the Holy Spirit had never *descended and remained* on a person before. In the Old Testament, the Holy Spirit had descended on a number of people such as King Saul and King David, but He had never *remained*. These verses clearly indicate that the Holy Spirit descended and remained on Jesus. These verses also tell us that *Jesus baptizes with the Holy Spirit and fire.*

We've now read in all four Gospels that baptizing us in the Holy Spirit is a ministry of Jesus. So I must ask you: If that is so, why would you *not* ask Jesus to baptize you with the Spirit? If you've given your life to Him, entrusted Him with your future, sing songs at church about how much you love and trust Him—why would you not say, "Lord Jesus, please baptize me with the Holy Spirit"?

Jesus' Example

Let's approach this question another way. I'm sure you would agree that Jesus is our example. So, does He offer a pattern for us to follow in this matter? Let's see!

First of all, did Jesus get born again? Technically, no. Jesus was the first and only person since Adam's fall who didn't need to be born *again*, because He was born right the first time. You and I, on the other hand, were born wrong the first time, so we need to be born again. Jesus was born a child of God. We need to be born again to become children of God. He is our example.

Second, was Jesus water baptized? Yes! We know that Jesus was baptized by John in the Jordan River.

Third, was He baptized in the Spirit? As a matter of fact, the Bible makes it plain that He was. Here's what the Word says happened immediately after Jesus was baptized in water:

> Then Jesus, when He had been baptized, came up immediately from the water; and behold, the heavens were opened to Him, and He saw the Spirit of God descending like a dove and alighting upon Him. And suddenly a voice came from heaven, saying, "This is My beloved Son, in whom I am well pleased"(Matt. 3:16-17).

Many people read this passage and come away thinking that a literal dove floated down onto Jesus. They apparently miss the words that make it clear that it is a *simile*—"like a" dove. It was the Holy Spirit that descended on Him!

From that day forward, Jesus began to do miracles. He began to operate in power. Later, He told the disciples, "Don't you begin your ministry until the Holy Spirit descends on you. You won't accomplish anything without the power of the Holy Spirit" (see Luke 24:49).

Some people think the words of the Great Commission ("go into all the world and preach the gospel") were the final words of Jesus on Earth. They are indeed important words; however His final instructions before His ascension to heaven were not to "go," but to "stay." Stay in Jerusalem until you receive the baptism in the Holy Spirit.

> And being assembled together with them, [Jesus] commanded them not to depart from Jerusalem, but to wait for the Promise of the Father, "which," He said, "you have heard from Me; for John truly baptized with water, but you shall be baptized with the Holy Spirit not many days from now. . . . But you shall receive

power when the Holy Spirit has come upon you; and you shall be witnesses to Me in Jerusalem, and in all Judea and Samaria, and to the end of the earth" (Acts 1:4-5,8).

Foreshadowing from the Old Testament

Abraham

The story of the life of Abram (whom God later renamed "Abraham") shows us a type of baptism in the way God called him forth to a new life:

> Now the LORD had said to Abram: "Get out of your country, from your kindred and from your father's house, to a land that I will show you" (Gen. 12:1).

The calling of Abram out of his native land is a type of salvation. God was saying to Abram, "Come out from among them and be separate, and start following me." This call out of paganism and darkness was a foreshadowing of the salvation that would one day become available in Jesus.

Later, God instructed Abram to prepare a covenant ceremony, one in which an animal is sacrificed and cut lengthwise into two pieces:

> And it came to pass, when the sun went down and it was dark, that behold, there was a smoking oven and a burning torch that passed between those pieces (Gen. 15:17).

Although it may not be obvious at first, the cutting of flesh and passing through it was actually a type of water baptism. (Remember that Romans 6 likens water baptism to a spiritual form of circumcision.)

First Corinthians 10 likens water baptism to the crossing of the Red Sea. What happened when Israel crossed the Red Sea? There was a cutting (parting) of the sea, then a passing through. Then the enemy (Egypt) who was pursuing them was left in the sea! In the same way, God wants us to leave the "old man" in the water of baptism.

So far, we have Abram symbolically receiving the baptism of salvation through being called out of his native country. And we have him being symbolically baptized in water through the "passing through" of the covenant cutting ceremony of animal flesh. So, it shouldn't surprise us to also find a type of Holy Spirit baptism in Abram's life. We find it in Genesis 17:5:

> No longer shall your name be called Abram, but your name shall
> be Abraham; for I have made you a father of many nations.

Compare the two names. Two letters are added to the name "Abram" to create "Abraham"—the letters A and H. This is the Hebrew root word 'ah which, in the Old Testament, is used to refer to breath, or the breath of God, spirit, or the Spirit of God, or the Life of God.[5] Just pronouncing the word gives you the sense of breath or wind. If you draw it out as you say it you get "aaaaahhhhhhh," and you hear the sound of breath—the unmistakable indicator that a person is a living spirit.

'Ah is also part of the Hebrew compound word ru'ah which is also used many times in the Bible to describe the life-giving breath or Spirit of God.[6] Ru'ah is the word translated "Spirit" in Genesis 1:2, where we read, "And the Spirit of God was hovering over the face of the waters." A few verses later, we find 'ah again when God creates Man:

> God formed man of the dust of the ground, and breathed into
> his nostrils the *breath* of life; and man became a living being
> (Gen. 2:7, emphasis added).

Simply put, the Hebrew word 'ah speaks of God's animating, empowering Spirit. So isn't it interesting that God would say, "No longer shall your name be Abram, but from now on your name shall be called Abr-*ah*-am. God put His "breath" inside of Abram's name as a type and sign of this third baptism that he needed. Abraham was never the same after that day.

Here's an interesting side note. God knows that it can often create friction in the home when one spouse is baptized in the Holy Spirit and the other isn't. So what did God do for Abraham's wife, Sarai?

> Then God said to Abraham, "As for Sarai your wife, you shall not
> call her name Sarai, but Sarah shall be her name (Gen. 17:15).

This is a beautiful type of the baptism in the Holy Spirit. In Sarai's name,
God takes out the selfish "I" and replaces it with the "ah" of His Spirit.

Using my imagination a little bit, I can see Abraham out there just
worshiping God, when suddenly the Lord announces, "I'm changing your
name. It's not going to be Abram anymore, it's going to be Abraham."
Then God breathes on Abraham—"aaaahhhhh"—and Abraham feels a
breeze of power and love blow through him. He has been baptized in the
Holy Spirit (and so his name declares it!) A little later in the conversation
God says, "We're going to have to do something about Sarai too." She is
over in the house washing the dishes when suddenly a wind blows
through the kitchen. She feels the Spirit of God fill her being. And her
husband starts pronouncing her name differently.

Do you see it now? Even the life of Abraham foreshadows the three
baptisms.

Ezekiel

Once I overcame my previous indoctrination and got baptized in the
Holy Spirit, I read through the whole Bible looking for types and symbols of this experience in Scripture. I was astounded by how many symbols there were.

For example, I remember reading through the book of Ezekiel and
thinking, *I probably won't find any types of this baptism here.* As you may
know, Ezekiel is a very unusual prophetic book. There is a lot of proph-
esying of doom and destruction (Ezekiel is pretty much mad at everyone), and lots of measuring things (in visions Ezekiel always seems to be
measuring stuff). I doubted that I would find any symbolic types in this
book. Then I came across Ezekiel 16:9.

Do you remember the three things that "bear witness" on the earth?
The blood, the water, and the Spirit. Keep them in mind as you read this
verse:

Then I washed you in water; yes, I thoroughly washed off your blood, and I anointed you with oil.

In the Bible, oil is frequently a symbol for the Holy Spirit. Here we have water, blood and an anointing with oil—the three baptisms.

Now let's read a bit in 1 Corinthians 10. Paul writes:

Moreover, brethren, I do not want you to be unaware that all our fathers were under the cloud, all passed through the sea (v. 1).

Here Paul is referring to the series of events in which Moses led the children of Israel out of Egypt, with a cloud of God's power and presence leading them miraculously through the Red Sea. In the Old Testament, Moses is a type of Christ. He was a deliverer who led God's people out of bondage, foreshadowing that Jesus would deliver us from slavery to sin and death. As a matter of fact, one of the earliest Old Testament prophecies about the Messiah connects Moses to Jesus (see Deut. 18:15-18).

With that in mind, let's go back to 1 Corinthians 10 and read verse 2: "All were baptized into Moses in the cloud and in the sea."

Paul says the children of Israel had three baptisms: into Moses; in the cloud; and in the sea. Is that not clear? They were baptized into their deliverer Moses (a type of salvation); they were baptized "in the sea" when they passed through the Red Sea (a type of water baptism); and they were baptized "in the cloud"—a cloud being another symbol for the power of God's Spirit.

If you study the Tabernacle that God instructed the children of Israel to build while they were in the wilderness, you see another Old Testament portrayal of the three baptisms: There was an Outer Court; within that was "the Holy Place"; and within that was "the Holy of Holies"—where the presence of God dwelt.[7]

As believers, what part of the Tabernacle should we desire to inhabit? Not the outer court, far from the power and presence of the Lord, but in the Holy of Holies, right? Well, please take note that there were three things you would have had to do before you could go into the Holy of Holies as the high priest.

The first thing you would have encountered upon entering the Tabernacle would have been an altar. There you would have sacrificed a spotless lamb, shedding its blood. Would you like to take a guess at what baptism that represents? The baptism of salvation, of course.

Next, you would have gone to a laver, a type of basin containing water. There you would have carefully washed and purified yourself. Of course, this closely parallels water baptism. But there was one more thing you would have *had* to do before you could enter the Holy of Holies and experience the full glory of the presence of God. You would have had to be anointed with oil. Failure to take this step would have resulted in the priest dropping upon encountering God's glory.

Before you could enter the presence of God, you would have had to have the blood, the water, and the oil. Keep in mind that this meticulous process wasn't cooked up by some ancient priest. God Himself gave the detailed instructions for it to be done just this way.

I don't care who you are, but you simply cannot say, "Yes, Lord, I want to be saved. Yes, I want to be water baptized. But I'll pass on that Holy Spirit baptism part, because I've heard that can make you do weird stuff." And why would you even want to say that to Him?

God's Word is undeniably clear here. If you want to enjoy the fullness of God's power and presence then you need to be baptized in His Holy Spirit.

A Changed Life

When Jesus ascended to heaven, He sent the Holy Spirit to baptize us, fill us, empower us, help us, comfort us and lead us into all truth. When you are Spirit-baptized, you receive power to walk in your new life. (By the way, that includes empowerment to control your tongue!) You are able to live in a way that truly testifies to God's supernatural power.

I am a walking, talking testament to that transforming power. If you doubt me, I suggest you go back to the town where I grew up and tell the police department that Robert Morris is a Christian now and is the pastor of a church. Do you know what they would say? "There is a God!"

The three baptisms I've experienced bear witness to the supernatural. Here's how all three baptisms work together.

When you are saved, you become a new person.

When you are water baptized, the old person gets cut off.

When you are Spirit baptized, you receive power to walk in a new life.

Perhaps now you're beginning to realize why there are so many defeated Christians. I see so few who are truly living victoriously, because they were saved later in life and have never been water baptized. On top of that, they have accepted a doctrinal system that tells them they don't need baptism in the Spirit. As a result, they continually struggle. They fail and they fall. They pray and then see very little in the way of results.

These three things bear witness on Earth: the blood, the water and the Spirit—salvation, water baptism and Spirit baptism.

Ask and You Shall Receive

If you're wondering, *Does it have to happen in that order? In other words, is it possible to be baptized in the Holy Spirit before being baptized in water?* I believe the answer is yes. I believe this because in Acts 10, the Gentiles were saved, *then* baptized with the Holy Spirit, *then* water baptized. (We Gentiles always seem to get things mixed up! But it's okay with God.)

Salvation, however, is a prerequisite to the other two. You can't be baptized in the Holy Spirit if you've never been cleansed and spiritually reborn through the baptism into Jesus. It's simply not possible. I've met many people who were baptized as children but who were actually truly saved only later in life—as teenagers or adults. Such people need to be baptized in water to be fully obedient to the Lord's instructions.

There is no escaping that these Scriptures beg for a decision to be made. The question is, Will you embrace the power and provision God has made available for you to live a victorious life, or will you cling to a doctrinal tradition and remain at basically the same spiritual level?

Baptism in the Holy Spirit is a separate experience from salvation. It is a simple thing to receive. In fact, all you have to do is pray and ask for it.

But Robert, you may be thinking, *shouldn't I be afraid to open myself wide to an outpouring of the Spirit's power and influence? After all, what if I accidentally open myself up to some sort of demonic influence?*

Those are common questions. I'll let Jesus answer them for you.

> If a son asks for bread from any father among you, will he give him a stone? Or if he asks for a fish, will he give him a serpent instead of a fish? Or if he asks for an egg, will he offer him a scorpion? If you then, being evil, know how to give good gifts to your children, how much more will your heavenly Father give the Holy Spirit to those who ask Him! (Luke 11:11-13).

Serpents and scorpions are biblical symbols for demonic powers. Jesus made that clear in Luke 10 when He told His disciples, "Behold, I give you the authority to trample on serpents and scorpions, and over all the power of the enemy, and nothing shall by any means hurt you" (v. 19).

Jesus was telling them not to be afraid of asking the Father for the Holy Spirit. He would give the Spirit freely. And when He did, it would be good for them. They would like it!

So what are you waiting for? Ask Him! The only thing you have to lose is powerlessness, defeat and frustration. One thing you will gain—among many other wonderful benefits—is the ability to get your tongue under control and into the service of heaven. That's quite a deal.

Notes

1. Charles Grandison Finney, *The Autobiography of Charles G. Finney* (Bethany House Publishers, 1977), n.p.
2. R. A. Torrey, *Why God Used D. L. Moody* (World Wide Publications, 1992), n.p.
3. Ibid.
4. Ibid.
5. H. W. F. Gesenius, *Gesenius' Hebrew and Chaldee Lexicon to the Old Testament* (Grand Rapids, MI: Baker Book House, 1984).
6. Ibid.
7. Alfred Edersheim, *Bible History, Old Testament* (Grand Rapids, MI: William B. Eerdmans Publishing, 1995).

CHAPTER EIGHT

The Language of Heaven

We've been looking at how to engage the help of the Holy Spirit to tame our tongues. (In fact, He is our only hope of doing so!) Now that we have explored baptism in the Holy Spirit, let's look at one of its benefits—the fact that we can enter into the presence of God and allow the Holy Spirit to actually change our words. So isn't it interesting to consider the fact that one of the gifts of the Holy Spirit mentioned in the Bible is a gift called "tongues"? Is there any connection between allowing the Holy Spirit to change our words and the gift of tongues? You bet there is.

Any book that hopes to show you how to control the tongue must include a thorough discussion on the gift of tongues and "prayer language."

If you read through the book of Acts with fresh eyes and an open heart, you'll see that over and over, when people received the baptism in the Holy Spirit, they began to do what the Bible calls "speaking with tongues." In other words, what I have called "the baptism of heaven" was consistently demonstrated by speaking in "the language of heaven."

As part of this discussion of the widely misunderstood subject of tongues, I want to share a little bit of my own search for truth on this subject. Perhaps I know, as well as anyone, the controversy that surrounds it. Not only have I heard the reasons that *all* believers can't (or shouldn't) receive it, but at one time, I confidently preached a few of those reasons myself. As a matter of fact, one particular incident shows just how deeply my bias and misconceptions about tongues had been.

It Happened One Night

My wife, Debbie, had a wonderful smile on her face that Sunday morning as we were getting ready for church. She looked quite pleased and amused about something.

"What are you smiling about?" I asked.

"Oh, nothing."

"You don't have that grin on your face for nothing," I said. "Come on and tell me what you're smiling about."

"I don't want to embarrass you," she admitted.

Now my curiosity was really up. "Please tell me anyway," I coaxed.

"Well, last night I couldn't sleep, and I went into the living room to read my Bible for a while," she said. "When I came back into the bedroom, I heard you."

"Heard me doing what?"

"Well, I heard you praying in tongues."

The only problem with her statement was the fact that I didn't pray in tongues. I couldn't believe what she was telling me.

"What are you saying?" I asked her again.

"I heard you," Debbie replied. "Apparently you couldn't sleep either, so you were praying in tongues, and I heard you."

"No," I said. "I was asleep. Are you telling me the truth? Was I really praying in tongues last night?"

Her answer was yes.

. . . .

I relate that event because it so clearly shows what kind of resistance against praying in tongues I had built up in my mind. I couldn't pray in this way while awake! My spirit, however, wanted to pray so badly that I began praying in my prayer language while I was sound asleep!

If that sounds preposterous to you—I assure you that I understand!

For most of my Christian life, I did not believe that speaking in tongues was available or even desirable. In fact, at one point, I believed that tongues were of the devil! The denomination I had been associated with taught that the gift of tongues had passed away in the first century.

But eventually, like D. L. Moody, I began to encounter believers who clearly operated in greater dimensions of God's power and spiritual authority than I did. These men and women constantly had things happening around them that were similar to things I read about in the Bible—things that had supposedly "passed away" 1,900 years ago. This set me on a search of Scripture that ultimately led me to acknowledge, embrace and passionately desire the fullness of the Holy Spirit in my own life and ministry.

Once I finally got baptized in the Holy Spirit, I began to prophesy (another major gift of the Spirit), but I did not speak in tongues. Debbie, however, who received the baptism in the Holy Spirit about the same time I did, began speaking in tongues immediately.

What I didn't realize was that when I prayed to receive the baptism in the Holy Spirit and to speak in tongues—God answered my prayer! He hadn't withheld this wonderful gift from me. However, my mind wouldn't consciously allow my spirit to function in this way. But in my sleep, my spirit was able to bypass my mind, and I prayed in tongues freely.

Speaking in tongues is such a tremendous blessing in my life that I have a desire for *every* believer to have this experience. If you haven't yet received this gift, I want you to know that you can.

If there is a question in your mind about whether or not speaking in tongues is available to you, I encourage you to prayerfully read on and consider the scriptural evidence. Look carefully at each passage—then decide for yourself.

(Warning: A *lot* of Scripture is about to come your way. Some passages are lengthy. Please don't let that intimidate you. It's vitally important that you see how truly biblical all of this is. In fact, perhaps you should see it in your own Bible. Feel free to look up each passage cited to see it in your preferred translation.)

The True Gift Is the Spirit

Before we dive into the verses that speak directly of the phenomenon of tongues, let's stop here for a moment and remember what the gift of the Holy Spirit is. Many people miss this important truth: The gift of the Holy Spirit *is* the Holy Spirit. (Read that sentence again.) Tongues (and other manifestations) are included in this gift. But as we read in the previous chapter, the actual gift is the Person of the Spirit.

To illustrate my point, let's say that I gave you the gift of an expensive Swiss watch. Would the minute hand be included in that gift? Of course! I wouldn't give you the watch without the minute hand. I'd give you the whole watch, and the minute hand would naturally be part of the gift.

In the same way, speaking in tongues is naturally part of the baptism in the Holy Spirit. It is one, but by no means the only, indicator that a person has received the gift of the Holy Spirit. It is a gift that Jesus told His followers to expect.

> Nevertheless I tell you the truth. It is to your advantage that I go away; for if I do not go away, the Helper will not come to you; but if I depart, I will send Him to you. . . . However, when He, the Spirit of truth, has come, He will guide you into all truth; for He will not speak on His own authority, but whatever He hears He will speak; and He will tell you things to come. He will glorify Me, for He will take of what is Mine and declare it to you (John 16:7,13-14).

Jesus emphasized this promised gift right before He ascended into heaven:

> And being assembled together with them, He commanded them not to depart from Jerusalem, but to wait for the Promise of the

Father, "which," He said, "you have heard from Me; for John truly baptized with water, but *you shall be baptized with the Holy Spirit not many days from now.* . . . But you shall receive power when the Holy Spirit has come upon you; and you shall be witnesses to Me in Jerusalem, and in all Judea and Samaria, and to the end of the earth" (Acts 1:4-5,8, emphasis added).

In essence, Jesus told them, "Make sure you don't leave Jerusalem until you get the Holy Spirit, because when He comes, you will have the power you need to be effective witnesses for Me." True to His promise, a few days later, 50 days after Jesus' death, the Helper arrived.

> Now when the Day of Pentecost had fully come, they were all with one accord in one place. And suddenly there came a sound from heaven, as of a rushing mighty wind, and it filled the whole house where they were sitting. Then there appeared to them divided tongues, as of fire, and one sat upon each of them. And they were all filled with the Holy Spirit and began to speak with other tongues, as the Spirit gave them utterance (Acts 2:1-4).

The promised gift had arrived—the One whose presence Jesus said would be so beneficial that it would be better for the disciples than having Jesus Himself remain with them. The disciples were filled with the Holy Spirit and spoke with other tongues. Jesus said they would, and they did. He also said they would receive power to be witnesses, and was this ever true!

Peter walked into that upper room with his confidence shattered by his threefold public denial of Jesus a few weeks earlier. He walked out of that room a fearless spokesman for the brand-new gospel. He boldly proclaimed that gospel, and 3,000 people were saved that day. The next day, 5,000 were saved. Not only that, but there were many signs and wonders.

> Then those who gladly received his word were baptized; and that day about three thousand souls were added to them. And they continued steadfastly in the apostles' doctrine and fellowship, in

the breaking of bread, and in prayers. Then fear came upon every soul, and many wonders and signs were done through the apostles (Acts 2:41-43).

Do you think the devil was happy about this? I think he was terrified! This was an unprecedented threat to his kingdom. When Jesus was on the earth, the threat to Satan's kingdom was isolated to one geographic spot—wherever Jesus happened to be standing. Now millions of little Jesuses could be empowered and could spread all over the planet! Whoever received this Helper that Jesus had sent could do the same things Jesus had done, which Jesus predicted: "Most assuredly, I say to you, he who believes in Me, the works that I do he will do also; and greater works than these he will do, because I go to My Father" (John 14:12).

This is why the devil immediately began plotting how to stop people from receiving this gift. What was his strategy? Creating controversy; he endeavors to convince people that this gift is not for today—that it has passed away. If that doesn't work, He tries to make people believe that it is only available to a select few. He has even gone so far as to take credit for it by trying to get Christians to believe praying in tongues is of the devil!

The truth is, power from on high through the baptism in the Holy Spirit was and is available to believers. The enemy was and is desperately trying to stop believers from receiving it.

But he couldn't do it then; and unless we buy the lies, he can't do it now.

In Acts 10, we read that Peter received a vision from the Lord that communicated to him that the gospel of Jesus Christ was not for the Jews only but was also for those who were non-Jews, the Gentiles. As a result of this vision, Peter preached to Cornelius's household and made a startling discovery. Not only was salvation made available to the Gentiles, but also the baptism in the Holy Spirit! Here's what happened:

Then Peter opened his mouth and said: "In truth I perceive that God shows no partiality. But in every nation whoever fears Him and works righteousness is accepted by Him. . . ." While Peter was still speaking these words, the Holy Spirit fell upon all those who heard the word. And those of the circumcision who believed

[Jewish believers] were astonished, as many as came with Peter, because *the gift of the Holy Spirit had been poured out on the Gentiles also. For they heard them speak with tongues and magnify God.* Then Peter answered, "Can anyone forbid water, that these should not be baptized who have received the Holy Spirit just as we have?" And he commanded them to be baptized in the name of the Lord (vv. 34-35,44-48, emphasis added).

Notice that Scripture says the Jews were *astonished* that the gift of the Holy Spirit was poured out on the Gentiles. I imagine they had already built a doctrine in their minds that this gift of God was reserved for the Jews alone. They had probably decided that only a select few could receive it.

The Lord, however, made it plain that the gift of the Holy Spirit is for everyone. Notice also what it was that made it so clear to everyone that these Gentiles had received the gift of the Holy Spirit: "For they heard them speak with other tongues and glorify God." Speaking in tongues was one of the unmistakable signs they had come to associate with Holy Spirit baptism.

So, in Acts 10, these disciples found out that God shows no partiality in dispensing the Holy Spirit and His gifts. Then in Acts 19, it is recorded that the apostle Paul confirmed this truth. He discovered that the gift of the Holy Spirit was still available years after the Day of Pentecost, years after Peter preached to Gentiles at Cornelius's house. Years later, Paul, while visiting Ephesus, found some disciples and said to them:

"Did you receive the Holy Spirit when you believed?" So they said to him, "We have not so much as heard whether there is a Holy Spirit." And he said to them, "Into what then were you baptized?" So they said, "Into John's baptism." Then Paul said, "John indeed baptized with a baptism of repentance, saying to the people that they should believe on Him who would come after him, that is, on Christ Jesus." When they heard this, they were baptized in the name of the Lord Jesus. And when Paul had laid hands on them, the Holy Spirit came upon them, and they spoke with tongues and prophesied (vv. 1-6).

The gift of the Holy Spirit was still available to believers—years later. It did not—and has not—passed away. When these people received that gift, they spoke with tongues and prophesied.

That same gift and *language* of the Holy Spirit is available to you.

Getting a New Glossary

You may have never thought of the fact that "tongues" is a language. But that is what the apostle Paul calls it in 1 Corinthians 13:1. I realize that Paul's primary focus in this passage was to help us understand that walking in love is more important than anything else. But for the purpose of our study, I want to point out that the word translated "tongues" in this Scripture is the Greek word *glossa*, which basically means "a language." It's the source of our English word *glossary*, which refers to a collection of words and terms.

Paul says, "Though I speak with the tongues [language] of men and of angels, but have not love, I have become as sounding brass or a clanging cymbal." In making his point, Paul was revealing his awareness of a heavenly language, the "tongues" of angels.

Another important reference regarding the *language* of tongues is found in the account of the Day of Pentecost, which we've read partially. Let's consider Acts 2:4-6 in the light of the thought that tongues is a language.

> And they were all filled with the Holy Spirit and began to speak with other tongues, as the Spirit gave them utterance. Now there were dwelling in Jerusalem Jews, devout men, from every nation under heaven. And when this sound occurred, the multitude came together, and were confused, because everyone heard them speak in his own language. Then they were all amazed and marveled.

Notice that when tongues were being *spoken*, languages were being *heard*.

The language of tongues, while unique, also holds many of the same characteristics as other languages. Let me explain by addressing some of the myths often associated with tongues.

Myth: You Speak in Tongues with Immediate Fluency

When a child first begins talking, does he speak fluently the first day? Is his enunciation correct from the onset? Does he initially have a full vocabulary?

The answer to all these questions is, "No, of course not!"

When you begin speaking in tongues, it's as if you are learning a language for the first time. You won't speak fluently, perfectly or have an educated vocabulary the minute you receive this gift. But that's okay! You will grow in this gift just as you would in any other gift (e.g., teaching, leading, giving).

Just as you thrilled at every sound your child made when he or she began to speak, God loves to hear every syllable you say. Did it matter to you that your child sounded inept? No—to you it was beautiful! That's the way God feels too.

For instance, our son used to call the glove compartment the glove department. He called it that for years. Eventually he said it correctly, but until that time we just enjoyed hearing him say glove department. We thought it was cute. I'm sure similar stories come to your mind about your own children.

The point I'm trying to make is that tongues, in a sense, is a language you *learn*. You become fluent in your prayer language the same way you become fluent in any other language.

Myth: You Can't Control Speaking in Tongues

Some people mistakenly believe that this language is just going to pop out of you. I know, because I was one of those people! I thought that if I was supposed to speak in tongues, it would happen automatically. Looking back, I see how absurd that thinking was.

Let me assure you that you are in control of the use of your prayer language the same way you are in control of the use of any language or, for that matter, the use of any other spiritual gift. For example, people who have been baptized in the Holy Spirit never find themselves at the deli counter ordering a pound of sliced turkey when all of a sudden they begin uncontrollably speaking in tongues. That simply doesn't happen. Nor do people who have the spiritual gift of prophecy find prophetic utterances flying out of their mouths at inopportune times. You are in control. First Corinthians 14:32 (*AMP*) says it this way:

> For the spirits of the prophets (the speakers in tongues) are under the speaker's control [and subject to being silenced as may be necessary].

To further illustrate this point, let's suppose you had been given the gift of teaching. You wouldn't be at all concerned that you would involuntarily take the stage at your local Chuck E. Cheese's during your child's birthday party and start teaching an unruly preschool crowd the Four Spiritual Laws, would you? Certainly not! If that were to happen, it would be because you made a conscious decision to shout down the giant mouse on stage. A gifted teacher is always in control of when and how that gift is exercised.

The same principle is true for speaking in tongues. And what's more, if God has called you to teach His Word to an unsaved crowd, don't think that the first time you step into a pulpit you are going to sound like Billy Graham. It will take some time to develop any gift God gives you!

You are in control of when and how you use and develop the gifts God gives you. Keep in mind too that it takes effort and practice to become proficient at anything you do—including speaking in tongues.

The Language of the Spirit

Praying in tongues also takes faith. It is the language of the Spirit, not of the natural world. Because of this, your mind, which is part of your soul, will not understand it.

First Corinthians 14:2 tells us, "He who speaks in a tongue does not speak to men but to God, for no one understands him; however, in the spirit he speaks mysteries."

Why is it that no one but God can understand a man who prays in tongues? Because, as I said, it is the language of the Spirit. Therefore, only the Holy Spirit understands it. First Corinthians 14:14-15 states this in a nutshell:

For if I pray in a tongue, my spirit prays, but my understanding is unfruitful. What is the result then? I will pray with the spirit, and I will also pray with the understanding. I will sing with the spirit, and I will also sing with the understanding.

Please look at these verses very, very carefully.

Paul makes it clear that when he is praying in tongues, his spirit is praying. Then he asks, "What is the result?" He says he will pray with the spirit (in tongues) as well as with his understanding. In accordance with the two contrasting types of prayer Paul outlines in this passage, are you praying in the spirit in addition to praying with your understanding?

Paul goes on to explain why both are important: "If I pray in a tongue, my spirit prays, but my understanding is unfruitful" (1 Cor. 14:14). We understand with our minds, with the intellect. But the apostle Paul wanted you and me to know that we are *never* going to understand praying in tongues with our natural minds. Never. However, verse 13 in that same chapter tells us that we can pray for an interpretation to the tongues we speak. We can pray to understand the interpretation with our minds. It says: "Therefore let him who speaks in a tongue pray that he may interpret."

Paul is letting us know that our minds are not going to understand it when we pray in tongues unless God gives us the interpretation.

The conclusion? We need to do both. We need to pray in tongues and pray with our understanding.

Okay, now let's take a pop quiz. When you pray with your understanding, are you praying with your spirit or your soul? When you pray in tongues, are you praying with your spirit or your soul?

Hopefully those questions were a snap to answer: You pray out of your soul (because your mind is part of your soul) when you pray with your understanding. You pray out of your spirit when you pray in tongues. In light of that, let me ask you this: How many prayers have you prayed that were soul-ish prayers rather than spirit-breathed prayers?

Sobering, isn't it?

One huge advantage to praying in the spirit is the fact that when you pray in this way, you are praying the perfect will of God for the situation. You are praying prayers of the Holy Spirit. You are not praying what you hope is the answer. Rather you are praying God's solution.

The difference between praying with limited natural understanding versus praying in the spirit might be compared to walking alone on a dark, moonless night feeling your way step-by-step, timidly guessing if you are going in the right direction, versus having an experienced guide with a high-intensity outdoor floodlight showing you the way and revealing any pitfalls along the path. A guide with such a powerful light would help you reach your destination expeditiously.

That's what praying in the spirit can do for you! You hit the mark every time because you are allowing the Holy Spirit to guide you in your prayers and in your life. As we have already seen, John 16:13 tells us:

> However, when He, the Spirit of truth, has come, He will guide you into all truth; for He will not speak on His own authority, but whatever He hears He will speak; and He will tell you things to come.

What a marvelous promise!

Spiritual Weight Lifting

Praying in tongues as opposed to praying with your understanding has numerous benefits! In addition to those we've already discussed, praying in tongues actually strengthens you and builds you up. It helps you stay in shape spiritually.

Jude 20 says, "But you, beloved, building yourselves up on your most holy faith, praying in the Holy Spirit." According to this verse, praying in the Holy Spirit will strengthen—or build up—your faith. It is equivalent to spiritual weight lifting. As we just saw in 1 Corinthians 14:14-15, praying "in the Spirit" means praying in tongues.

If you've ever worked out, you know that strength training is done over time. You don't just waltz into the gym one day, pump some iron and walk out a world-champion weightlifter.

Physical exercise must become part of your daily routine if you hope to become physically fit. And it's worth the time it takes. Studies show that the benefits of exercise are numerous and can be quickly realized physically, as well as mentally and emotionally. Getting in shape helps you become more alert and produces endorphins that cause you to have a sense of well-being.

In the same way, the benefits of spiritual exercise are numerous! The results can be realized in your spirit, soul and even your physical body. You already know that you will receive power to be a witness for the Lord as a result of receiving the Holy Spirit. But you may not realize that as you spend time praying in the spirit, you'll find that you are more alert and tuned in to the Lord, His Word will become more alive to you, and your prayer life will be revolutionized. In addition, as Ephesians 6:18 says, after exhorting us about putting on the armor of God, praying in the spirit is vital in overcoming adversity, for if you are in the midst of a battle, "praying always with all prayer and supplication in the Spirit" is part of the arsenal you use to win!

When you spend time praying in the Spirit, you'll become more and more like Jesus in that you'll find yourself doing those things the Father would have you do (see John 5:19).

Praying in the Spirit is a wonderful, supernatural gift. I can't say enough good things about it. I would never want to do without it. And neither did the apostle Paul. He was keenly aware of the necessity of praying in tongues to stay spiritually strong. I believe that is evident when Paul said, "I wish you all spoke with tongues" (1 Cor.14:5).

Whoa. Let's stop right here a moment. Is the above statement in the Bible? (Perhaps you should check yours to make doubly sure.)

And who authored that statement? Paul penned it, but the author is the Holy Spirit; all Scripture is inspired by God (see 2 Tim. 3:16).

Thus, we have the Holy Spirit, through Paul, saying, "I wish you all spoke with tongues." The realization of this truth hit me so strongly one day that I have never forgotten it. If the Holy Spirit desires that *all* speak in other tongues, does that include you and me? Yes.

So, I would like to suggest that this Scripture might compel you to get over whatever hang-up you might have about the subject and open your heart and spirit to receive this.

Still not convinced? Then consider the apostle Paul's personal testimony. He said, "I thank my God I speak with tongues more than you all" (1 Cor. 14:18).

How important was praying in tongues to this man who wrote nearly one-third of the New Testament? According to this Scripture, it was of primary importance; it was part of his lifestyle. But wait—there's more! (As they say on infomercials!)

Let's find out what else Paul had to say on this subject. If you came from a denominational background as I did, I can well imagine you are anxious for me to do just that. In fact, I imagine that you may be thinking, *Hold on; you didn't read the rest of those verses. The ones where Paul talks about all the abuses of tongues that were going on.* Believe me, I'm familiar with all the objections you may have. Remember, I've been there, done that.

I'd like to bring to your attention the context in which the apostle Paul penned those words. You may not be aware that he was writing a *corrective passage* to the Corinthian church when he wrote those verses. This correction was necessary because they were praying in tongues at *inappropriate* times during a corporate church service. He was pointing out to them that when they were in that setting, it would be best to make sure that what they were saying and praying could be understood by those present, particularly when unbelievers were among them.

Although many people take this passage in 1 Corinthians 14 to mean that tongues are not important, or that praying in tongues is wrong, that is not at all what Paul is saying.

Let's read the first five verses of this chapter to clear it up:

Pursue love, and desire spiritual gifts, but especially that you may prophesy. For he who speaks in a tongue does not speak to men but to God, for no one understands him; however, in the spirit he speaks mysteries. But he who prophesies speaks edification and exhortation and comfort to men. He who speaks in a tongue edifies himself, but he who prophesies edifies the church. I wish you all spoke with tongues, but even more that you prophesied; for he who prophesies is greater than he who speaks with tongues, unless indeed he interprets, that the church may receive edification.

Take note. Paul says that the one who speaks in tongues "edifies himself." Do you know any Christian, including yourself, who has absolutely no need of being built up? Are you fully encouraged, completely at peace, and spiritually strong—all the time? Then perhaps you won't need to avail yourself of this amazing opportunity. The rest of us, however, are very much in need of a way to gain spiritual power and refreshing for spirit and soul. And God has provided it!

Praying in tongues is a great blessing. It is speaking mysteries to God and it edifies the person who is praying—but *only* the person who is praying. That was Paul's point. On the other hand, he says, giving a word of prophecy can edify everyone who hears it. That's why prophecy (or tongues with the interpretation which is equivalent to prophecy) is preferable in a corporate church setting.

Nevertheless, believers who pray in tongues aren't being selfish. On the contrary, they need to be built up and strong, precisely because they need to be able to encourage, help and minister to others. People who are beaten down, run down and drained are in no position to help anyone.

Paul continues to bring correction and instruction to the congregation at Corinth in verses 6 though 25. But notice, *never* does he discount the validity of praying in tongues. He is merely striving to bring order to an out-of-order situation that existed in this particular church.

He wraps up his discourse by saying:

Whenever you come together, each of you has a psalm, has a teaching, has a tongue, has a revelation, has an interpretation. Let all things be done for edification. If anyone speaks in a tongue, let there be two or at the most three, each in turn, and let one interpret. But if there is no interpreter, let him keep silent in church, and let him speak to himself and to God (vv. 26-28).

"Let all things be done for edification." That is the point.

There is nothing wrong with your edifying yourself by praying in tongues! In fact, it is definitely something you should do. I don't think

Paul could have stated the case more perfectly than when he said, "I wish you all spoke with other tongues."

Furthermore, verses 39 and 40 say, "Therefore, brethren, desire earnestly to prophesy, and do not forbid to speak with tongues. Let all things be done decently and in order."

"Do not forbid to speak with tongues," it clearly says. Entire denominations have lost sight of that verse! They have focused for so long on the "decently" and "in order" part that they've forgotten the "let it be done" part. In fact, they have done precisely what the Lord says not to do—that is, forbid people to speak with tongues.

And let's not forget that Jesus had something to say about this subject as well. He said:

> And these signs will follow those who believe: In My name they
> will cast out demons; they will speak with new tongues (Mark
> 16:17).

In some of His final words, Jesus said that speaking with tongues is a sign that follows believers. Notice the requirement mentioned here. In order to cast out demons *and* speak with tongues, what must you do?

Be a believer—believe, have faith.

A Pure Language

One day, as I was reading my Bible, the Lord showed me something else about praying in this new language, which was one of the most exciting things I've ever seen in Scripture. I was reading the story about the Tower of Babel, which may be a familiar passage to you. It begins in Genesis 11:1 with this: "Now the whole earth had one language and one speech."

Have you ever wondered what language they were speaking? I don't know that we could say with certainty, but we could surmise that they were speaking the same language that Adam and Eve had spoken in the Garden of Eden. It stands to reason that when God created mankind, He gave them a language, and from that time until the time of the Tower of Babel, the population of the whole earth spoke this one language.

When sin came on the scene, however, that language became a problem. We know this because when people with sinful natures began building a tower to heaven,

> The LORD came down to see the city and the tower which the sons of men had built. And the LORD said, "Indeed the people are one and they all have one language, and this is what they begin to do; now nothing that they propose to do will be withheld from them. Come, let Us go down and there confuse their language, that they may not understand one another's speech." So the LORD scattered them abroad from there over the face of all the earth, and they ceased building the city. Therefore its name is called Babel, because there the LORD confused the language of all the earth; and from there the LORD scattered them abroad over the face of all the earth (Gen. 11:5-9).

Picture a primitive people making adobe bricks by hand and stacking them one at a time high into the atmosphere. How could they engineer the thing to reach to heaven? I mean, how could they have achieved such an impossible feat? Why didn't God just let them continue to *try* to build that tower clear up to His throne room? Think about it. Not even today's technology has allowed us to reach into heaven. Yet Scripture indicates they could have pulled it off.

It also tells us why it was possible. They could have done it simply because they spoke the same language! With that one language, nothing they proposed to do would be withheld from them. With that one language, they could achieve anything—even the seemingly impossible.

That was a dangerous ability to be entrusted to sinful mankind. Therefore, the Lord took that ability away from them by confusing their language.

Okay, now for the really good part. Are you ready? That day while I was reading those verses in Genesis, the Holy Spirit brought to my remembrance another Scripture—Zephaniah 3:9:

> For then I will restore to the peoples a pure language, that they all
> may call on the name of the LORD, to serve Him with one accord.

Notice in this verse, God says He was going to *restore* a language, not that He was going to *give* the peoples a language. God is going to *restore* a "pure language" to the peoples.

What language do you suppose He is referring to?

There is only one language that is pure—it's the language of heaven, or the language of the spirit. I believe this for a number of reasons.

For one thing, every other language has been defiled. Every language has profanity, obscenity and uncleanness mingled in it. Not only that, but the book of Zephaniah is speaking prophetically about Jesus, the Messiah, coming into the earth. In light of that context, this Scripture is promising a pure language to a *redeemed* people. Only those who believe in the Lord Jesus Christ are redeemed.

In essence, when we consider Genesis 11 and Zephaniah 3 together, we see that God is saying, "People can't have this pure language (and ability) with their sinful nature, but once I send my Son and redeem them and change their nature to be a holy nature, I can give back to them (restore) this language (and ability). This language will make them one with My Holy Spirit, and nothing they propose to do will be withheld from them."

Remember, the purpose of this language according to Zephaniah 3:9 is "to serve Him with one accord." In light of that, let's read Acts 2:1,4 again:

> Now when the day of Pentecost had fully come, they were all
> with one accord in one place. . . . And they were filled with the
> Holy Spirit and began to speak with other tongues.

Isn't it amazing that it tells us they were "with one accord"? Zephaniah 3:9 predicts that when this pure language is restored, we will serve Him "with one accord"—the same words used in Acts 2!

I'm convinced that speaking in tongues is the pure language of the spirit. It causes believers to be in one accord so they might serve the

Lord! I also believe it is God's desire that we all speak with the heavenly language when we're baptized in the Holy Spirit. That's the way it happened in the account recorded in the book of Acts. Unfortunately, doctrinal error often hinders people from being able to readily receive it. (Ask me how I know!)

This is what I've discovered: Speaking in tongues is a language—a wonderful, remarkable, unique language that transcends *any* and *all* barriers. It's a heavenly language that allows you to have direct communication with the Father.

This language is available to believers—to you—right here, right now.

If you're a Christian and would like to receive it, you can. The only requirement is that you believe. Just ask for the baptism in the Holy Spirit as explained in the previous chapter and then step out in faith. Please understand though, that you will have to step out. Contrary to many people's preconceived notions, you're not going to fall into some sort of trance and begin babbling uncontrollably. The Spirit is not going to take control of your will. You will have to make the conscious decision to move your tongue and utter sounds—allowing the Holy Spirit to pray through you.

If you will, the benefits are numerous. As you give the Holy Spirit control of your tongue, your words will begin to line up with God's Word. Your life will begin to line up with God's will for your life.

Why is this so vital? Because your words set the course of your life. What better way to set your course than to speak with a pure language—the language of the spirit? What better way to tame your tongue than to *yield* it every day, by a choice that you make, to the only One who has the power to tame it?

Yes, the only hope we have of taming our tongue and halting the hurt, destruction and death it can cause is with the aid of the Helper—the Holy Spirit—whom Jesus sent to put God's words of truth in our mouth.

WORDS

CHAPTER NINE

The Gates of Praise

Praise is God's address; it's where He lives. So, if you want
to be where God lives, you have to offer Him praise.
DEREK PRINCE

It is my incredible privilege to be the founding pastor of a wonderful congregation in the Dallas-Fort Worth area in Texas. Since we began the church several years ago with a handful of friends, we've seen extraordinary blessing, fruit and increase. Today we have the honor of bringing thousands of believers together each weekend for uplifting worship and exploration of God's Word.

Of course, once I was certain that God was leading me to start a church, one of the first big decisions I had to make was what the name should be. After much prayer, the Lord led me to a passage of Scripture that provided the ideal name for our new fellowship—one that captured our vision, mission and call.

The passage tells of the patriarch Jacob on a journey, sleeping out under the stars one night. In a spot he would later name Bethel, which means "house of God," Jacob had a breathtaking dream in which he saw a multitude of angels moving between Earth and the throne of God in heaven:

Then Jacob woke up and said, "Surely the LORD is in this place, and I wasn't even aware of it." He was afraid and said, "What an awesome place this is! It is none other than the *house of God*—the gateway to *heaven*!" (Gen. 28:16-17, *NLT,* emphasis added).

Thus, with the Lord's prompting and blessing, we named our new work Gateway Church. Our vision and hope was that it would be known as a place where people hungry for more intimacy with God would find it— that it would be a gateway to an eternal relationship with the heavenly Father. And if you ask around our community, I believe you'll find that God has honored that desire.

I love helping people discover the joy, peace and power that comes from spending time in the presence of God. It's one of the greatest thrills of my life and calling. Of course, the first prerequisite for experiencing God's presence is being born again and, with my evangelistic gifting, I get a great deal of joy out of introducing people to the One who makes a relationship with God possible—Jesus Christ.

Once you have been made spiritually alive through faith in Jesus, you will not automatically experience God's presence in fullness and power all the time. There is a gateway to the highest levels of His presence.

How to Pass Through the Gates

As we learned at the very beginning of this study, words are connectors not only to people but to God as well. That's why no study of the power of words would be complete without an examination of the most powerful and amazing thing your words can do. I'm talking about bringing you into close proximity to the majestic, all-powerful Creator of the universe. (And if you didn't know, that's a very good thing!)

The kind of words I'm referring to are words of *praise*. Such words are a literal gateway into God's throne room. Isaiah 60:18 makes this connection when it says, "You shall call your walls Salvation and your gates Praise." Notice that *gates* are referred to as *praise* in this Scripture. However, there is more than one setting in which you can pass through those gates.

Opening the Gates Corporately

Have you ever heard the terms "corporate prayer" or "corporate worship"? I'm not referring to a Fortune 500 company getting "religion." The word "corporate" means "a group of people coming together to do something in a united way." Corporate worship and praise is a very biblical concept. Throughout the Bible, we see that God's people are encouraged to enter His presence corporately, through the gates of praise. For example, we find this kind of encouragement beautifully illustrated in the familiar words of Psalm 100:4:

> Enter into His gates with thanksgiving, and into His courts with praise. Be thankful to Him, and bless His name.

This verse was addressed to an assembled group of worshipers in Israel during King David's time. But it is just as valid for us today. If you are in a congregation that is actively praising and worshiping the Lord through music, you may have experienced how easy it is to sense God's presence during those times. You know the Lord is near you, and you can feel His love. He may even speak to your heart or touch your physical body with healing as you praise and worship Him.

Without a doubt, entering into the presence of the Lord can be achieved through thanksgiving and praise. Praise connects you to everything that God is—your Redeemer, your Healer, your Defender, your Peace, and so much more. Why is praise such a gateway to God? Psalm 22:3 tells us:

> But thou art holy, O thou that inhabitest the praises of Israel (*KJV*).

When we corporately praise the Lord (as Israel did), He shows up and inhabits our praises and makes Himself known to us. It's no wonder that we often sense His beautiful presence when we come together in worship!

Opening the Gates Individually

Here's more great news. We don't have to wait for a Sunday service to connect with God and experience the refreshing that comes from His presence. We can go through the gates of praise as individuals, in our own private times with the Lord. It isn't difficult to communicate with Him. After all, the very Spirit of God dwells within us as born-again believers. First Corinthians 6:19-20 says:

> Or do you not know that your body is the temple of the Holy Spirit who is in you, whom you have from God, and you are not your own? For you were bought at a price; therefore glorify God in your body and in your spirit, which are God's.

Because God's Spirit dwells within you, you can worship Him any time, any place—and He will inhabit your praises!

The Word makes it clear that sincere "praisers" always get the Lord's attention. But you would look through the Bible in vain for any evidence that grumbling or complaining is a gateway to anything but self-pity. Only thankful people can march right into His courts and come into His presence through those gates of praise.

What happens when you enter into God's presence? Psalm 16:11 tells us of some of the benefits of being vitally connected with the Lord:

> You will show me the path of life; in Your presence is fullness of joy; at Your right hand are pleasures forevermore.

Doesn't that sound appealing? "Fullness of joy"! Everlasting "pleasures"! These are the things you find in God's presence. Yet Satan has actually persuaded people to be afraid of God's presence. He's done a brilliant job of convincing even mature believers that God is mad at them, and any time spent in His presence will probably be filled with the opposite of pleasure and joy—condemnation, criticism and rejection.

Of course, the devil is a liar. But how tragic it is that so many of God's children have been deceived into fearing Him. I can testify from years of personal experience that there is great joy in God's presence. It's good there. And the more fully you experience it, the more you want!

The fact is that every need in your life can be met in God. No matter what circumstance or situation you find yourself in, all you really need to do is to connect with the heavenly Father, who loves you, through the words you speak to Him.

For instance, if you are in debt, you need to get in His presence and find out His wisdom for financial freedom. If you are addicted to drugs, alcohol, tobacco or pornography, you need to be in His presence, where you will find power to break that hold on your body and soul. If you are on the brink of divorce, you need to be in His presence and obtain His grace and help to save your marriage.

God's manifest presence in your life is *the* answer in these and all other situations you may be facing. It is an awesome thing to realize that you can enter into God's presence through the gates of praise and receive what you need from Him.

So why not set aside a period of time today—and every day—just to worship and praise Him? Think about the fact that you have the ability to enter into His presence and experience fullness of joy. Think about the fact that you can draw close to Him and be encouraged, comforted, helped and blessed. It's easy! Just open your mouth and step right through the gates of praise.

Speaking Life

Your words are gate-openers. When you speak, you either open a gate of praise for God to walk through or you open a gate of hell for the enemy to walk through. "Gate opening" isn't optional. The only question is, *Which* gate will your words open?

If you open the gate of praise, God comes on the scene and brings life. So, if there's a sick person who needs to be healed, a mountain that needs to be moved or a sea that needs to be parted—the One who can do all those things shows up when your mouth agrees with the Word of God.

If your mouth speaks things contrary to the Word, you open the gate for the devil to come on the scene—death, disease, destruction, defeat, discouragement and depression follow him.

Let's come full circle in this study. Remember the verse with which we started?

A man's stomach shall be satisfied from the fruit of his mouth, and from the produce of his lips he shall be filled (Prov. 18:20).

If you ever meet a truly satisfied person, you can know that person is speaking right things. That person is consistently speaking words of life from God's Word.

The converse is also true. If you ever meet a person who is not satisfied with life, it's because his or her mouth isn't lining up with God's Word. Take a look at the very next verse, our keynote Scripture in this study:

Death and life are in the power of the tongue, and those who love it will eat its fruit (v. 21).

Let's break down that verse and answer a question that nagged me for quite a while when I first began studying and preparing this teaching. The verse says, "Those who love *it* will eat *its* fruit."

Love what? What does *it* refer to?

There are several possible answers to this question. We could say *it* refers to death: Those who love *death* will eat the fruit of death. Or, we could say *it* refers to life: Those who love *life* will eat the fruit of life. Then again, we could say *it* refers to the tongue: Those who love *the tongue* will eat the fruit of the tongue.

In my opinion, none of those answers is correct. I believe that *it* is referring to the *power* of the tongue.

That being the case, we could read Proverbs 18:20 this way: "Death and life are in the *power of the tongue* and those who love [respect, honor or embrace] *the power of the tongue* will eat the fruit of it." I think that's a fair paraphrase of that verse and is consistent with the truth the Lord wants us to receive from it.

In other words, if we understand the *power* our words carry; if we understand the *power* that is present in our words of praise, we will experience the results of that *power*.

What Happens When We Agree with God

When I earnestly sought the Lord for understanding of this Scripture, I received a revelation that I believe you will appreciate. Before I explain it to you, let me first ask you this question: Do we have the power to create life with our mouth?

Many charismatic Christians would probably answer yes. However, I don't believe yes is the correct answer. The reason I say that is because only God, who is *the* Creator, has the power to create life. The Creator, however, has given you and me the power to agree with Him and speak His Word, thereby facilitating *His* life with *our* words.

Can you see the difference? God's Word is life. Proverbs 4:20-22 says so:

> My son, give attention to my words; incline your ear to my sayings. Do not let them depart from your eyes; keep them in the midst of your heart; for they are life to those who find them.

If your words agree with His Word, the Lord comes on the scene and life is created. On the other hand, if your words agree with what the enemy wants to see happen in your life, you can be certain he'll be there, before you can turn around twice, to work toward bringing the destruction you've spoken from your mouth.

The devil just loves to hear people say things such as

· My marriage will never succeed.
· We'll never get out of debt.
· These kids are driving me crazy!
· My husband will never get saved.

These kinds of words are just what your enemy is longing to hear! He's standing ready to help these things come to pass—count on it. Life *and* death are in the power of your tongue.

When we agree with the Creator's Word and speak those things out of our mouths, the Creator will see to it that those things come to pass. In John 14, that's just what Jesus says:

> Do you not believe that I am in the Father, and the Father in Me? The words that I speak to you I do not speak on My own authority; but the Father who dwells in Me does the works (v. 10).

Jesus spoke the words He heard His Father say, and His Father did the works. In the same way, the Bible is God's Word to us. If we say what we hear Him say in the Bible, then the Father—the Creator—will do the work.

Let me give you an illustration. Let's say that a man comes to me after a church service and says, "Pastor Robert, please pray for me to receive healing." When I pray with him he gets healed.

Did I heal him? Of course not. *God healed him.* I merely prayed for him. I just said the things I've heard my Father saying in His Word. God, the Creator, has the power of life. So when we agree with God, we receive life in our marriages, our families, our finances, etc. If we don't agree with God, we receive the opposite. We must come into agreement with God; His presence does the miracle.

Here's another verse that clearly represents this principle but has, in my opinion, often been misunderstood:

> Again I say to you that if two of you agree on earth concerning anything that they ask, it will be done for them by My Father in heaven. For where two or three are gathered together in My Name, I am there in the midst of them (Matt. 18:19).

Contrary to popular belief, it is not the agreement that brings the miracle. The operative words in the verse above are "for" and "by." It's not done *by* them *for* the Father. It's done *for* them *by* the Father. The Father is the one doing the work! This explains *why* there is power in agreement. Words of agreement bring God on the scene. And when God shows up, supernatural power shows up. Wasn't that true in the life of Jesus when

He walked on the earth? When He showed up, powerful stuff happened! His presence was characterized by signs, wonders and miracles.

Formerly blind Bartimaeus would tell you that was true after Jesus restored his sight! The woman who only touched the hem of Jesus' garment and "was made well from that hour" (Matt. 9:22) wouldn't hesitate to tell you that *only* Jesus had the power to heal her. The multitudes who witnessed Jesus take five loaves and two fish and feed them all would tell you there was supernatural power in His presence.

The list could go on and on. Both the Old and New Testaments are filled with accounts of God's supernatural power at work. It's natural for God to be supernatural. The key is getting Him to show up. And the way we get Him to show up is to agree with His Word and praise His name. Our mouths bring in the presence of God and the presence of His power.

Psalm 50:23 says it this way: "Whoso offereth praise glorifieth me: and to him that ordereth his conversation aright will I show the salvation of God" (*KJV*).

God desires to bless you. He desires to answer your prayers. He desires to give you the desires of your heart. You need only get into His presence and receive from Him. And, as we've already discussed, there is a correct way to enter into His presence—through the gates of praise. Your words are the key.

Speaking the Language of Praise to Others

We've seen how pivotal our words are when approaching God. Now, let's talk for a moment about their importance when dealing with people.

First, because you all people have been created in the image and likeness of God, it shouldn't come as a shock that many of the same principles related to approaching God can apply to our human relationships.

Do you think that when you approach someone in an angry, mean spirit that you will cause him to listen to you favorably? Of course not. Just the opposite is true. When you approach someone in a spirit of love and praise, that person is more likely to listen to you and receive what you have to say or help you with your request.

Thus, praise not only opens the gate to God's presence, it also opens the gate to people.

Praise to Our Spouse

If you are married, I'm sure you know what I'm talking about. For instance, if a wife would like her husband to take out the trash, she needs to ask him in the correct way *if* she wants to get positive results. Nagging probably won't get the job done. Complaining about it certainly won't get the trash out to the street either. But if the request is made in the right spirit, or in the right way, that man will take the trash out and possibly do the dishes too!

Of course, the same principle applies when a husband communicates with his wife.

More often than not, when there is a breakdown in communication, it is not that what is being said or requested is *wrong*, it is that it's being said in a *wrong manner. How* we say what we say is important. And because we are made in the image of God, people are more likely to receive what we're saying and grant our request if our words are coated in love, honor and respect.

I believe the virtuous woman spoken of in Proverbs 31 understood and practiced this principle of communication. If you read the story, you find that it basically chronicles this woman's virtues. In Proverbs 31:23, right in the midst of the list of her accomplishments, we read:

> Her husband is known in the gates, when he sits among the elders of the land.

It's an amazing thing to me that in this passage of Scripture not one word is mentioned about the character of this woman's husband. Proverbs 31 talks about her character and accomplishments, which leads me to conclude that her husband's success was considered one of *her* accomplishments.

I can just imagine this young couple walking by the city gates arm-in-arm. Each time they stroll by, this prudent wife whispers in her husband's ear, "You're going to sit there in those gates one day. I believe in you. You're a great man of God. You're a wise and wonderful man. One day you'll be a respected elder."

I think this virtuous woman made it a point to build up her husband and praise him. I suspect it was her words that got God involved and brought life to her husband and to their future. I imagine that her words had everything to do with her husband's success.

We all need to hear that we have value and that someone believes in us. It encourages us to continue to do well. Mark Twain spoke for a lot of men when he said: "I can live for two months on one good compliment!"

Sincere compliments, or praise, energize us. If you doubt that is true, think about the last time you received praise of any kind. How did it affect you? What were the results of your receiving that praise? What reactions have you received when giving praise to others?

We need to remember that we have the ability to praise our spouses and help them become the people God created them to be.

Praise to Our Children

Speaking the language of praise to your children will work wonders for them as well! That's why it's important to look for opportunities to give them sincere praise. When you speak words of praise, God comes on the scene.

In his excellent book *The Five Love Languages of Children*, Gary Chapman says this about words of praise and encouragement:

> Such words are like gentle warm rain falling on the soul; they nurture the child's inner sense of worth and security. Even though such words are quickly said, they are not soon forgotten. A child reaps the benefits for a lifetime.[1]

It's important to praise our children for their effort, as well as for their accomplishments. How many times have you been faced with a difficult task, only to ultimately prevail just because you knew how to stick with it? Teach your son or daughter that winners never quit. Praise your child as he or she learns to stay the course.

Even the secular sources have discovered and validated this biblical principle. Check out this observation from *Psychology Today*:

> Grit may turn out to be at least as good a gauge of future success as talent itself. In a series of provocative new studies at the University of Pennsylvania, researchers find that the gritty are more likely to achieve success in school, work and other pursuits—perhaps because their passion and commitment help them endure the inevitable setbacks that occur in any long-term undertaking. In other words, it's not just talent that matters but also character.[2]

Help your children develop the character they need to succeed in life. Praise them for making a sincere effort, even if they do poorly. Praise them into trying again and persevering until they achieve the results they're after. Even when your children do things wrong, speak to them in positive terms. Let them know that you believe in them—that you believe they are good children.

For example, you can say something like, "I know you're a great child, so why would you strap your little brother to the car with duct tape? That's not like you!"

Believe the best in them—that's the way God does it. He believes the best in us. That doesn't mean there shouldn't be correction applied for wrongdoing, because children need to know there are consequences for bad behavior. But they also need to know that you love them and have confidence in them, no matter what!

Learn to speak the language of praise over your children—it's the language of life.

Overcoming Life Situations

Praise also opens another very important gate—the gate to God's power. We find this principle in Isaiah 61, a passage of Scripture that gives us an amazing prophetic glimpse into the scope of Jesus' power and ministry. The third verse in this chapter gives us further insight into the power of praise. It says the promised Messiah will be sent

To console those who mourn in Zion, to give them beauty for ashes, the oil of joy for mourning, the garment of praise for the spirit of heaviness; that they may be called trees of righteousness, the planting of the LORD, that He may be glorified.

Let's focus on the revelation that Jesus gives us "the garment of praise for the spirit of heaviness." That is especially good news today. According to the National Institutes of Health:

Depression is increasingly common in the United States and internationally. Approximately 18.8 million American adults, or about 9.5 percent of the U.S. population age 18 and older in a given year, have a depressive disorder.[3]

Why is this so? Because there is a spirit of heaviness in the earth today. The enemy is pushing people down and trying to keep them down—in other words, he is de-pressing them. Do you know the primary way he does this?

Through words.

As a matter of fact, people can talk themselves into a full-blown state of depression. I think most people would admit to having done this at one time or another. I know I have. Do you ever remember speaking doom and despair over a situation? Did you realize at the time that you were inviting a spirit of depression to settle into your life?

Thank God that He has given us Isaiah 61:3 as the prescription for that condition! Speaking words of life and singing praises to God will put depression on the run. The enemy can't stay in the presence of God; and when you speak God's Word and sing praises to Him—God comes on the scene and depression has no choice but to take a hike!

According to the Bible, putting on the *garment* of praise is the antidote for the spirit of heaviness. As believers, you and I have a responsibility to consciously put on praise, much like we get dressed in the morning. Praise should be part of our wardrobe. If we'll get into the habit of praising the Lord each day, and periodically throughout the day, that spirit of heaviness won't be able to light anywhere near us.

You may be familiar with the Scripture in Ephesians 6 that exhorts us to put on the whole armor of God, that we may be able to stand against the enemy (see v. 11). In that passage, we are told to put on the helmet of salvation, the righteous breastplate, to shod our feet with the gospel of peace and to take up the sword of the spirit. We are to get dressed in this way because:

> We do not wrestle against flesh and blood, but against principali-ties, against powers, against the rulers of the darkness of this age, against spiritual hosts of wickedness in the heavenly places. Therefore take up the whole armor of God, that you may be able to withstand in the evil day, and having done all, to stand (vv. 12-13).

I would highly recommend adding the garment of praise to this daily attire for the same reasons listed here in Ephesians 6. The spirit of heav-iness is part of the devil's arsenal. If you are battling depression or men-tal problems, you are not fighting against flesh and blood; you are wrestling against spiritual wickedness.

Wear the Garment of Praise

God has given you a great way to win the battle! It's simple really. Just put on the garment of praise! Begin by praising God for saving you. Thank Him for what He has already done in your life. Praise Him for His good-ness and for what you anticipate He is going to do in your life. Continue to praise Him until the spirit of heaviness flees from you!

Remember, the power of life and death is in the tongue. And there is power in praise. When you speak life-giving words that agree with God's Word, God comes on the scene and brings life with Him. He's way big-ger than any demon! When He shows up, no demon is going to hang around!

It may seem hard to praise God when all you want to do is cry. At times it is a sacrifice to praise. That's why Hebrews 13:15 says, "Therefore by Him let us continually offer the sacrifice of praise to God, that is, the fruit of our lips, giving thanks to His name."

We need to praise God, *especially* when we don't feel like it. We need to praise Him especially when it's a sacrifice! We praise Him by faith! That is what will conquer feelings of depression. Words of praise bind the enemy. Words of praise open the gate to God's power.

Psalm 149 sums up the power of praise beautifully:

Let the high praises of God be in their mouth, and a two-edged sword in their hand, to execute vengeance on the nations, and punishments on the peoples; to bind their kings with chains [their kings of darkness, of lies, of unbelief, of fear, of cancer or whatever their fear is—to bind their king with chains] and their nobles with fetters of iron; to execute on them the written judgment—this honor have all His saints. Praise the LORD! (vv. 6-9).

When we enter into the gates of praise, we can execute judgment against our enemy! As the final verse of that psalm pointed out, this is an honor indeed. Of course, the greatest honor of all is the privilege of entering God's presence through the gates of praise. It is there that we will find fullness of joy and life forevermore! It is there where we can agree with the Creator of life and He can bring life into our every situation!

It is yet another amazing aspect of the power of our words.

Notes
1. Gary Chapman and Ross Campbell, M.D., *The Five Love Languages of Children* (Chicago: Northfield Publishing, 1997), p. 45.
2. Peter Doskoch, "The Winning Edge," *Psychology Today*, December 2005.
3. National Institutes of Mental Health (NIMH), "The Numbers Count: Mental Disorders in America: A Summary of Statistics Describing the Prevalence of Mental Disorders in America," 2001. http://www.nimh.nih.gov/publicat/numbers.cfm (accessed February 2006).

WORDS

CHAPTER TEN

Oh, How Much Your Words Matter!

As I believe you have seen throughout the pages of this book—and more important, within the pages of the Bible—your words matter more than you can imagine.

We have taken a tough but honest inventory of the negative and hurtful ways that we use our tongues. And we've seen how the Holy Spirit wants to partner with us to tame our tongues and turn them into powerful instruments of life, encouragement, hope and love.

Let me close our journey with an extraordinary example from the Bible and one very meaningful event in my own life. First let me show you a passage in the Gospels that sums up the whole theme of this book for me:

[Jesus] said to them, "But who do you say that I am?" Simon Peter answered and said, "You are the Christ, the Son of the living God." Jesus answered and said to him, "Blessed are you, Simon Bar-Jonah, for flesh and blood has not revealed this to you, but My Father who is in heaven. And I also say to you that you are Peter, and on this rock I will build My church, and the gates of Hades shall not prevail against it" (Matt. 16:15-18).

In the previous chapter, we discovered how to enter the gates of praise. In this passage of Scripture, Jesus speaks of storming the gates of hell. And in both cases, words are the key. He had just asked the disciples, "Who do the people *say* that I am?" The disciples responded, "Some *say* one of the prophets, some *say* Elijah, and some *say* John the Baptist." Then Jesus put them on the spot. "Who do *you say* that I am?"

Peter, inspired and enlightened by the Holy Spirit, declares, "You're the Messiah. The one we've waited for. The Son of God. I believe it!" This revelation filled his heart and then came out of his mouth. (Remember, out of the abundance of the heart the mouth speaks.)

Note what Jesus said upon hearing Peter's verbal profession. He pointed to Peter's words and said, "That's what I'm going to build my church on."

Keep in mind one of the primary truths we observed at the beginning of this study: Sin had created an enormous chasm between God and man. There was no way for us to bridge that gulf and get back to God. But He loved us so much, that He built the bridge. His name is Jesus. The Bible says, He sent His Word "and the Word became flesh" (John 1:14).

Now recall the words of Romans 10:9-10:

If you confess with your mouth the Lord Jesus and believe in your heart that God has raised Him from the dead, you will be saved. For with the heart one believes unto righteousness, and with the mouth confession is made to salvation.

Consider this wonderful truth in the light of Peter's revelation. Jesus had asked, "Who do you say that I am?" Peter's inspired response was,

"You're the Christ! You're the Son of the living God!" Here we have heart belief and mouth confession of Jesus as the Son of God and Savior. In other words, according to this passage in Romans, it appears that Peter became the first person on Earth to be saved!

Then Jesus said, "You're right! And let me tell you something else, Peter. You believed in your heart and you confessed with your mouth that I am the Son of God, and I'm going to build my church on that combination right there. I'm going to build a victorious, world-changing, glorious Church on people who will believe in their hearts and confess with their mouths. And hell itself will not be able to withstand the power of this dynamic combination."

Think about that. Hell cannot prevail against your step of heart belief and mouth confession of the Lordship of Jesus Christ. Satan simply can't prevail against that.

Words are so important. We must get our words lined up with the Word of God, because when we do, there is life in them.

Now I want to give you a specific example that is very meaningful to me.

In the second year after the founding of Gateway Church, our tiny staff was joined by an amazing young couple, Thomas and Mary Beth Miller. Both are extraordinarily gifted people—musically, artistically and spiritually. Thomas became our worship pastor and continues in that role to this day. We knew practically nothing about this couple when they came, other than the fact that God clearly had sent them to us. And what a blessing they have been to our fellowship and to the Body of Christ at large.

They hadn't been with us very long when, during one evening's worship service, something remarkable happened. Thomas was on the platform leading us in a very sweet time of worship in song and Mary Beth was one of the worship singers with him. We came to a point in which the presence of God was very tangible and thick. (Remember, praise is the gateway to God's presence!)

At that moment, I looked up at Mary Beth. She had a beautiful smile on her face as she was lost in worship. But as I looked at her, the Holy Spirit opened my eyes to something. I saw a spirit of death. More specifically, I saw a spirit of the fear of death.

It seemed to me that Mary Beth had, for a very long time, been battling the fear that she was going to die young. Keep in mind that at that moment, I had no natural knowledge of her past. I didn't know that her mother had died when Mary Beth was still a child. Nor did I know that Mary Beth had recently recovered from cervical cancer, a terrifying brush with a disease that had left serious medical doubts about her ability to ever conceive children.

Thus, I didn't know that in her mind she was carrying the nagging fear that she was going to die young too, until the Holy Spirit revealed it to me in that instant.

Later, when I took the platform to preach my message, Mary Beth had taken her seat on the front row. I looked at her and said, "Mary Beth, God has a word for you. He loves you and He comes tonight to break off from you a fear of dying young."

The tears that came instantly and powerfully to Mary Beth's face let me know that I had heard and seen accurately. I continued, "It's a spirit of fear, and it's not going to rule over you anymore. Listen. The Lord says, 'You are not going to die young. As a matter of fact, you're going to be a mother and a grandmother. Mary Beth Miller, you'll hold your grandchildren.'"

As I spoke those words to Mary Beth, belief rose up in her heart and jumped out of her mouth in a joy-filled confession, "I receive that! Thank you, Father!" Mary Beth will testify that the yoke of fear that had bound and tormented her for so many years was shattered that night. But that's not the end of the story.

On December 9, 2004, Mary Beth gave birth to a son, Thomas Harrison Miller III. A day later, Debbie and I visited Thomas and Mary Beth in the hospital and it was my privilege to hold that miracle in my arms and look into the sweet face of newborn life.

Please don't think that by sharing this story I'm congratulating myself or hoping that you will be impressed with my spiritual insight. It was simply my privilege that night in church to do what is available to every believer, including children and brand-new Christians. I simply heard from the Holy Spirit and spoke His word.

God used those words as a bridge to a hurting woman's heart. God brought life. And He created life.

The power of life and death is in your tongue. I pray that you will use it wisely. I pray that you will speak life over your family, your friends and your ministry. I pray that you will submit your tongue to the One who has the power to tame it—the Holy Spirit—and that you will avail yourself of the language of heaven to build yourself up for His service.

Finally, I pray that you will speak words that agree with God's Word. As we have seen, your words are either agreeing with God's, which have the power to bring life, or they are agreeing with Satan's. And he only wants to steal, kill and destroy. The choice is yours. With whom are you going to agree?

Yes, your words carry the power of life and death. What a responsibility! What a privilege!

The Power
The
Power
of Your
Words

For Further Thought
and Discussion

Preface

1. Read Genesis 12:3. Look for the "so that" clause. What was the ultimate purpose for which God blessed Abraham?

2. Now read 3 John 2. If you have prosperity, health and blessing in your life, what do you believe is God's ultimate purpose for blessing you with these things?

3. Read Deuteronomy 8:17-18. What is a mistaken idea about where wealth comes from? Where does wealth *really* come from, and what is the purpose of wealth?

4. Can you relate to the story about the explorer? Are there some truths in Scripture that you feel you have taken too far? Are there some that you need to learn more about?

CHAPTER 1

The Strength in a Word

1. How would you define a mouth that is like a "loaded gun"? When has your mouth been like a loaded gun? What kinds of scenarios cause you to shoot off your mouth?

2. Can you think of specific times when your mouth ever got you in trouble? What was the most painful time—either to you or to another person? Has your mouth changed since that time? Why or why not?

3. How have your words hurt your relationships with your family and friends in the past?

4. What do you feel that you can do to learn to control your tongue?

CHAPTER 2

Word Connections You Can't Live Without

1. Read John 1:1,14. How is Jesus, the Incarnate Word, the visible expression of the invisible God? How does He bridge the gap between the spiritual and the physical?

2. There's a lot about word-bridges in this chapter. What needs to happen in order for two living beings to get to know one another?

3. Words are spiritually powerful, a lesson not lost on Satan. According to Genesis 3:1-8 and Matthew 4:1-11, what is Satan's line of attack? Why does he start there?

4. Time for self-examination. If what Jesus said is true (and it is!) that "out of the abundance of the heart the mouth speaks" (Matt. 12:34), what has been coming out of your mouth lately? Blessings? Encouragements? Constructive coaching? Love? Curses? Discouraging words? Destructive comments? Bitterness? Take some time to pray right now, and then listen for God's reply to your heart. Record your thoughts below.

5. "Stop speaking death over your health, your finances, your marriage and your other relationships." How and when have you "spoken death" over these things in your life? Take some time to write down your thoughts about why this matters and how it affects your closest relationships.

6. "Start allowing your mouth to line up with the Word of God." Let's say that you've had a sudden sickness, or a sudden outflow of finances (or a slow-but-steady negative cash flow), or hit a rocky place in your marriage (or another relationship). What is your tendency to do in these situations?

7. How can you "speak life" to a situation that looks like "death"? Record your thoughts below.

CHAPTER 3

Can I Speak Freely?

1. If people spoke exactly whatever first came to their minds, what would the result be?

2. According to the scriptural principles in this chapter, what are appropriate constraints to put on your own speech?

3. Ephesians 4:25 says, "Speak truth to one another." But Job 6:25 says, "How painful are honest words!" If truth can be so very painful, what are we supposed to do? (Read Eph. 4:15).

4. Read Ephesians 4:15 again. If you can't speak the truth "in love," what should you do?

5. Think about the hurtful joking and "kidding around" you've experienced. What kind of joking is appropriate and what kind is inappropriate? Where do you draw the line? If you realize you've gone over the line, what should you immediately do?

6. In what way do our mean-spirited words last? Why is it so hard to forget spiteful, insulting things said to or about us? How can we get free from these "curses?"

7. When was the last time someone said some really life-giving, healing words to you? Have you had any moments like that—moments that were life-transforming? Record your thoughts below.

CHAPTER 4

Ten Deadly Sins of the Tongue

1. Do you have a problem with lying? (Be honest!) Have you made yourself accountable to a close friend in this area? If not, who could you
ask to be an accountability partner?

2. Can you identify a time when you have "sown discord" in the past?
How should you respond when someone who has a critical spirit
begins sharing with you?

3. Have you been a gossip? If not, can you think of times when you have
inadvertently spread gossip? How can you control this area of your life?

4. Have you ever shared information about someone or a situation that you found out later was not true? What would help you to avoid doing this in the future?

5. Have you ever shared something with someone else that was shared with you in confidence? What are some practical ways that you can become a trustworthy confidant?

6. Do you have a problem with cursing? If so, how can you break this habit in your life? Are you accountable in this area? Do you feel that you have spoken curses in the past that need to be repented of and broken?

7. Have you ever used God's name in a self-serving way? Describe what you did.

8. Do you have a tendency to use filthy speech? Is filthy speech used at the place where you work? How can you show love to unbelievers and yet avoid listening to filthy speech?

9. Are you a contentious person? Do you like to argue? Have you developed habits of being argumentative and contentious? How can you break these habits so they won't affect your relationships? Who is a trusted confidant that you could ask to help you in this area?

10. Are you a negative or a positive person? Have you developed a habit of speaking negatively? Is there a stronghold of unbelief in your life? What can you do to break this habit?

Optional Bonus Discussion Points on The Seven Deadly Sins

For those of you who liked to do extra credit in school.
(Guaranteed 'A'!)

Because many believers have little or no experience thinking about The Seven Deadly Sins, they are worth some attention. When we give some thought to these sins and the spiritual deficiencies in us that drive these sins, it can be a fruitful time for introspection and correction by the Spirit and the Word.

1. **Pride**. Read Proverbs 11:2. Why is pride "deadly"? Think of the first three of the Ten Commandments (see Exodus 20:1-7) and consider this question: Why would pride be first in the list of seven deadly sins? What is the chief spiritual element in pride? (Does being humble rule out having pleasure in one's accomplishments?) What character quality is the opposite of pride? How can we cultivate that quality? How would the use of the tongue relate to this character quality (and its opposite)?

2. **Envy**. Read Exodus 20:17. How are coveting and envy similar? What is the chief spiritual deficiency exhibited by someone who is consumed by envy or covetousness? What character quality is the opposite of envy? How can we cultivate that quality? How would the use of the tongue relate to this character quality (and its opposite)?

3. **Gluttony**. Read Proverbs 23:20. God has given us an appetite for food and drink. Why does God frown on gluttony? Read Matthew 11:19 and Luke 7:34. Does gluttony as a "deadly" sin rule out feasts and occasionally overeating? What is unseemly about someone who is made in the image of God indulging in food and drink in an unrestrained way? What character quality is the opposite of gluttony? How can we cultivate that quality? How would the use of the tongue relate to this character quality (and its opposite)?

4. **Lust.** The Seventh Commandment (see Exodus 20:14) is "Do not commit adultery." Now read Matthew 5:28. How did Jesus modify the original commandment? Did he nullify it, intensify it, or complete it by going back to its original intent? Sexual lust is a universal experience (especially among men). But now read 1 John 2:15-17. Here we see the concept of lust broadened to include a wider range of things than just sex. What kinds of things do you think this includes? What character quality is the opposite of lust? How can we cultivate that quality? And how would the use of the tongue relate to this character quality (and its opposite)?

5. **Anger.** The Sixth Commandment (see Exodus 20:13) is "Do not murder." Now read Matthew 5:21-22. How did Jesus modify the original commandment? Did he nullify it, intensify it, or complete it by going back to its original intent? Read Ephesians 4:26: Here we see that it is possible to be angry and yet not sin! However, now read James 1:20: Anger and wrath are very human emotions—but most of the time we're angry because our agenda, our wants, our desires have been blocked. How can we know the difference between righteous anger and unrighteous? What character quality is the opposite of lust? How can we cultivate that quality? And how would the use of the tongue relate to this character quality (and its opposite)?

6. **Greed**. The Eighth Commandment (see Exodus 20:15) says, "Do not steal." Greed is the "never enough" syndrome. Read Proverbs 11:6; Luke 12:15; Romans 1:29; Ephesians 5:3. What conclusions can you reach about greed from these passages? Why is God so against it? Now read Colossians 3:5. Why does Paul say that greed "is" idolatry? What character quality is the opposite of greed? How can we cultivate that quality? And how would the use of the tongue relate to this character quality (and its opposite)?

7. **Sloth**. Slothfulness is not mentioned in the Ten Commandments. Why do you think in the moral teachings of the Church that it is listed as the last of the Seven Deadly Sins? Slothfulness comes up in the book of Proverbs more than any other book (see Prov. 12:24,27; 15:19; 18:9; 19:15,24; 21:25; 22:13; 24:30; 26:13-14). What's the connection between lacking wisdom and slothfulness? Read Hebrews 6:12: What character quality is the opposite of slothfulness? How can we cultivate that quality? And how would the use of the tongue relate to this character quality (and its opposite)?

CHAPTER 5

The Troublesome Tongue

1. Even though our tongues are small members of our bodies according to the book of James, they can do a lot of damage. Has your tongue started some forest fires or caused some shipwrecks in your life and relationships? Take some time now to record names and events (if you feel uncomfortable doing that, use code words! The important thing is to bring them to memory so that you can start doing things differently).

2. Consider the 10 sins of the tongue. Which of these sins are you most likely to commit? How could learning to control your tongue make a difference in your life? In your family?

3. When you were born again, God gave you a desire to serve and follow Him. According to Romans 12:1-2, how important is it for us to renew our minds with God's Word? How will learning about controlling your tongue affect your life? (Record some specific ways.)

4. Were you affected by words spoken to you when you were growing up? How have those experiences affected the way you interact with people today? Have you forgiven those who spoke bad things to you? Write the names of the people that you need to forgive.

5. Are you focusing on what God's Word says about you and not on the negative words that people have spoken to you? What practical steps can you take to believe what God says about you?

6. How can you begin speaking life instead of death over your life? Over your friends? Over your family?

7. Proverbs 18:21 tells us: "Death and life are in the power of the tongue." Proverbs has *much* more to say about the tongue. Below are selected verses from Proverbs that tell us how words can heal and harm. Read these verses in one sitting and let them speak to your spirit. (You may want to pick out a couple of verses to memorize. Use your preferred Bible version; this version is *NKJV*.)

10:18   Whoever hides hatred has lying lips, And whoever spreads slander is a fool.

10:21   The lips of the righteous feed many, But fools die for lack of wisdom.

11:11   By the blessing of the upright the city is exalted, But it is overthrown by the mouth of the wicked.

11:13   A talebearer reveals secrets, But he who is of a faithful spirit conceals a matter.

12:14   A man will be satisfied with good by the fruit of his mouth, And the recompense of a man's hands will be rendered to him.

12:17   He who speaks truth declares righteousness, But a false witness, deceit.

12:22   Lying lips are an abomination to the Lord, But those who deal truthfully are His delight.

12:25   Anxiety in the heart of man causes depression, But a good word makes it glad.

15:1   A soft answer turns away wrath, But a harsh word stirs up anger.

16:27   An ungodly man digs up evil, And it is on his lips like a burning fire.

18:6   A fool's lips enter into contention, And his mouth calls for blows.

18:8   The words of a talebearer are like tasty trifles, And they go down into the inmost body.

26:28   A lying tongue hates those who are crushed by it, And a flattering mouth works ruin.

29:20 Do you see a man hasty in his words? There is more hope for a fool than for him.

30:32-33 If you have been foolish in exalting yourself, Or if you have devised evil, put your hand on your mouth. For as the churning of milk produces butter, And wringing the nose produces blood, So the forcing of wrath produces strife.

8. Which verses jumped out at you? Use the space below to record what you hear God telling you through His words of wisdom.

CHAPTER 6

Taming the Tongue

One of the main points of chapter 6 is that "bridling" the tongue means to *pause, ponder* and *pray*. Let's consider each:

1. **Pause**. There's an old adage that if you feel anger, count to 10 before you open your mouth. Has that worked for you? If not, what are you personally going to do to buy some time before you say something you'll regret?

2. **Ponder**. Read 2 Samuel 16:5-10. When Shimei openly cursed David, David could have gotten offended and with a wave of his hand had Shimei's head removed from his shoulders. But look at the story. How did David respond? A lot of times, someone will say something to us that angers us *and it has some truth to it*. We want to get all defensive and insist that we're right, or that we're not doing anything wrong. But if we allow the Holy Spirit to speak to us through that person, we might learn something important. Can you think of any incidents in your own life where you have missed such an opportunity to hear from the Lord? Record your thoughts.

3. **Pray**. Controlling the tongue requires a prior work of God in our lives as well as attentiveness to the "voice" of God through the Word and through others who are speaking the Word to us. What does prayer have to do with all this? Can we expect to live a supernatural life without prayer? How can you build into your prayer life a way to listen for the still, small (or the loud, insistent) voice of the Lord in your life?

4. Another key point in this chapter is chopping down the tree of bitterness. Read Hebrews 12:14-15. What do you think is meant by the "root of bitterness"?

5. When Isaiah came into the Lord's presence (see Isa. 6:1-8), he was convicted of his words, and the Lord cleansed his mouth. How can you enter the Lord's presence every day? Are you committed to spending time with God every day? What needs to change in your schedule for this to happen?

6. Since the Bible tells us that we think in our hearts, do you remember a time when your heart was telling you to do something and you didn't do it? What were the consequences? What are some ways that you can train yourself to listen to your heart?

CHAPTER 7

The Baptism of Heaven

1. What is the Baptism in the Holy Spirit?

2. Have you received the Baptism in the Holy Spirit? How can you know if you have received the Baptism in the Holy Spirit?

3. Is there resistance or openness in your church to the Baptism in the Holy Spirit? Are there misconceptions about it? What are they?

4. How important is it to be filled with the Holy Spirit—to be "baptized" in the Holy Spirit?

5. Are you accustomed to reading Scripture in this way, or is it new to you? Be assured that this way of reading Scripture has an ancient pedigree going all the way back to Christ's own teachings about Himself in the Old Testament. (Read Luke 24:27,32.) The Church has come to call this way of reading the Scriptures "reading the Old Testament Christologically." Can you think of other picture-story/types of Christ in the Old Testament?

6. Under the subhead "Foreshadowing from the Old Testament," Abraham's life shows us *types* of baptism. Normally when we read "types" in our minds, we think of "kinds of." But "type" is a technical word in Bible study. It means pictures of future things to come. "Types of Christ" (foreshadowings of Christ) in the Old Testament include the entire sacrificial system (see Hebrews 8-10); the "three-day" journey mentioned in Genesis 22 in which God told Abraham to take "your son, your only son" Isaac up to a "mount" and "bind" him on the "wood" so that he'd become a "burnt-sacrifice offering (i.e., sin offering)." This picture-story, while not exactly prophecy, blazes a way for us to recognize that in Christ, who is God's son, a greater sacrifice happened on the Cross to take away our sins.

All this background is given to set up the following question:

What do you think of the threefold foreshadowing/fulfillment theme between Abraham's three "baptisms" and the three baptisms we are to have, culminating in the Baptism in the Holy Spirit?

CHAPTER 8

The Language of Heaven

1. How important is an ongoing, passionate relationship with the Holy Spirit to our ability to live the Christian life successfully? What are some areas of your life in which you've experienced spiritual growth through the power of the Holy Spirit?

2. In what types of experiences have you had difficulty controlling your tongue?

3. What are the myths about praying in a prayer language?

4. Isn't it amazing that there is a gift of tongues in the Bible? If praying in the Spirit builds us up and strengthens us, should we submit our tongues to the Holy Spirit on a daily basis?

5. Is it difficult for you to walk in the power and gifts of the Holy Spirit? Based on what you have read in this book, what can you do to build your faith in this area?

6. Have you received a prayer language from the Holy Spirit? Did you have to step out in faith when you received it? If you haven't prayed in a prayer language yet, are you willing to trust God in this area and yield your tongue to Him? If there is fear in your heart when it comes to the gifts of the Holy Spirit, will you ask the Lord to help you in this area?

7. What are some gifts of the Holy Spirit that you have already seen manifested in your life? (i.e. teaching, leading, giving, prophecy, faith . . .)

8. According to 1 Corinthians 14:14-15, what does Paul say about praying in tongues?

9. If this is a gift of the Holy Spirit that builds us up and strengthens us, what do you think Satan's agenda is? What tactics does he use?

10. First Corinthians 14:39 tells us not to forbid (people) to speak with tongues. Is this Scripture still relevant to us today?

11. What should be our attitude toward Christians who don't believe this gift is for today?

12. Why do you think there is so much controversy surrounding praying in tongues?

13. Since the power of life and death is in our tongues, is it important that we submit our tongues to the Holy Spirit every day so that we can speak life and not death? What are some practical ways that we can yield our tongues to God every day?

CHAPTER 9

The Gates of Praise

1. How do we enter God's presence with our words?

2. How do our words help us to speak to people who are created in God's image?

3. How is praise important to our daily lives? What are some of the most meaningful ways that you praise God?

4. When we are going through difficult times and we choose to praise the Lord with our words, how does this action help us?

5. Is there a specific time in your life when you remember God helping you through a difficult time because you chose to praise Him? Record your thoughts.

6. Do we have creative power? Is it God who has creative power, and when we choose to praise Him, is it His power that is released in our lives?

7. Are we trying to get God to agree with our words or are we trying to get our words to agree with God?

8. How does Satan try to get us to speak death over our lives and others?

9. How important are our words to life and blessing or death and destruction being released in our lives?

10. How important is the language of praise in our relationship with the Lord? How important is the language of praise in our relationship with our family and friends?

11. What does the Bible tell us about "putting on the garment of praise?" What are some ways that you can "put on the garment of praise" every morning?

CHAPTER 10

Oh! How Much Your Words Matter!

1. According to Romans 10:9-10, how are we saved? What do these verses say it is important to do with our hearts and our mouths?

2. How is believing in our hearts and confessing with our mouths important in our lives as believers? How is it important to our maturity and growth as believers?

3. What practical steps can you implement today and every day to help your words agree with God's Word and will for your life?